Doomed by Hope

About Masrah Ensemble
Masrah Ensemble is a nonprofit organization that makes, curates, develops, and fosters research and criticism of theatre with a focus on the Arab stage. Based in Beirut, Lebanon, the Ensemble aims to reconfigure audiences and to encourage transcendent, riveting theatre.

This book received generous and dedicated support from the **Prince Claus Fund.**

The **Young Arab Theatre Fund** provided a grant to subsidize translation costs.

Doomed by Hope

Essays on Arab Theatre

Edited by Eyad Houssami, Masrah Ensemble

Foreword by Elias Khoury

First published 2012 by Pluto Press
345 Archway Road, London N6 5AA

www.plutobooks.com

Distributed in the United States of America exclusively by
Palgrave Macmillan, a division of St. Martin's Press LLC,
175 Fifth Avenue, New York, NY 10010

British Library Cataloguing in Publication Data
A catalogue record for this book is available from the British Library

ISBN 978 0 7453 3355 7 Hardback
ISBN 978 0 7453 3354 0 Paperback

Library of Congress Cataloging in Publication Data applied for

This book is printed on paper suitable for recycling and made from fully managed and sustained forest sources. Logging, pulping and manufacturing processes are expected to conform to the environmental standards of the country of origin.

10 9 8 7 6 5 4 3 2 1

Designed and produced for Pluto Press by Chase Publishing Services Ltd
Typeset from disk by Stanford DTP Services, Northampton, England
Simultaneously printed digitally by CPI Antony Rowe, Chippenham, UK and Edwards Bros in the United States of America

Contents

Acknowledgments

Eyad Houssami

To the artists and scholars who fill the pages of *Doomed by Hope: Essays on Arab Theatre* with knowledge, stories, and insight, I extend my sincere thanks and gratitude. Their trust, rigor, and imagination never ceased to inspire me. I am indebted to theatre scholars Drs. Marie Elias, Marvin Carlson, and Nehad Selaiha for offering their mentorship, without which this book would never have come to fruition. They lent their expertise and guidance to the project at its inception and, as the core editorial review committee, provided authoritative feedback to the first drafts of the essays.

I am thankful to the Prince Claus Fund for granting the institutional and generous financial support that enabled the publication of *Doomed by Hope*. Albert Ferré, as the managing editor of the Prince Claus Fund Library, saw the potential of the project in late 2008. For more than three years, he advised me in my quest as an editor. Cora Taal, Keefe Cordeiro, Joumana El Zein Khoury, Fariba Derakhshani, and Christa Meindersma, director of the Prince Claus Fund, all buoyed the project with their administrative support and partnership as well as their unwavering faith in its promise. I feel fortunate to have teamed up with such an outstanding institution and warm community.

Given the bilingual nature of the book, authored and edited in Arabic and English in tandem, I have had the privilege of working with copy-editors, translators, and readers whose intellectual prowess and critical commentary served to hone and sharpen the substance of the content. English copy-editor Sophie Perl handled each text with the precision of a clockmaker, and Arabic-to-English translator Meris Lutz navigated diverse writing styles to achieve an idiom apposite to the tone of *Doomed by Hope*.

English-to-Arabic translator Sahar Mandour muscled through academic articles with cool alacrity, and Arabic copy-editor Mohammad Hamdan polished texts efficiently. Samar Awada translated the call for papers, numerous administrative documents, and the book's introduction, and she became a chief creative and intellectual collaborator through the process. Her versatility and work ethic were humbling. I am thankful also to Ahmad Moghrabi for his translation assistance and to writer and translator Fadi Tofeili and translator Suneela Mubayi for their astute recommendations throughout the editorial and translation process.

The readers, including Hussam Itani, Dalal El Bizri, Alexander Borinsky, Vasiliki Touhouliotis, and Sophie Perl, offered incisive anonymous commentary on the essays. Their questions and observations challenged the writers to re-evaluate the structure of their arguments and contours of their narratives and, in turn, to revise the essays with an invigorated sense of direction. Jowe Harfouche doubled as a translation consultant and external reader. He maneuvered between languages as he cross-checked translations with a fine-tooth comb, helping to align meanings and interpretations in order to ensure the integrity of translations.

Photo editor and photographer Dalia Khamissy took the painterly portraits of artists and theatre institutions in Syria, Lebanon, and Egypt and commissioned the images from Palestine and California that form the visual context of the book. I am thankful to Dalia for her commitment to achieving coherence and depth in the photography.

I am grateful to David Shulman, assistant commissioning editor at Pluto Press, for adopting the project and steering the final phase of the publication process. I have enjoyed the exchanges and conversations and feel privileged to have partnered with such an intelligent and enthusiastic publisher.

Dozens of other individuals, too many to name here, helped shepherd the book from one phase to the next. Christine Tohme, who opened the doors of the Ashkal Alwan archive to me for an undergraduate research project in 2006, encouraged me to reach out to the Prince Claus Fund, and Malu Halasa, Todd Reisz, and Manal Khader offered essential words of wisdom about publishing. Attoney-at-law Maya Mansour, producer Abla Khoury, and photographer Nadim Asfar each contributed unique professional expertise at pivotal moments of the process. With their recommendations and encouragement, Allan Hodgson and Katrin Saadé-Meyenberger as well as Khaled and Mona Malas were also helpful. In addition, I thank André and Lynn Gaspard of Saqi Books for their consideration of the project.

Thanks also go to the Young Arab Theatre Fund, in particular administrators Nicole Kayal, Jumana Al Yasiri, and Tarek Abou El Fetouh, for the grant that subsidized some of the translation expenses of the book. Likewise, I acknowledge the contribution of the Sharjah Art Foundation for inviting me to participate in the 2011 March Meeting, where I launched the call for papers for *Doomed by Hope*. As a fellow of the Fulbright US Student Program in 2007, I was able to live for one year in Damascus, Syria, where I had the wonderful opportunity not only to make theatre in Arabic and stage a performance art piece, but also to improve my Arabic language skills, engage with the repertoire of Saadallah Wannous, meet theatre artists and scholars, and formulate the premise of this book.

Were it not for the professors and theatre collaborators with whom I worked as an undergraduate at Yale, I would have never believed in the possibility of transnational theatre research and practice, an idea and phenomenon that is fundamental to this book. My gratitude to professors Toni Dorfman, Deb Margolin, Joseph Roach, Elizabeth Kassab, Jill Lane, Hala Nassar, and Ala Alryyes only deepens with time, for it is they who embraced and challenged the lines of academic and artistic inquiry that I hope have coalesced – at least for now – in *Doomed by Hope*. I am equally grateful to theatre artists and collaborators Clare Barron, Alexander Borinsky, and Daniel Kluger for nearly a decade of conversations, debates, and friendship, which has indelibly marked how and why theatre matters to me. The principles that emerged from these dialogues have no doubt shaped my approach to this book.

Finally, my sister Liane, brother Zeid, sister-in-law Lyn, parents Yazan and Rima, and great-aunt Hiam have been a source of endless support through thick and thin. I am especially thankful to my parents for making a contribution to supplement the translation budget. Five years ago, when I left the United States for Syria to embark on a life of theatre grounded in Arabic, they may have humored me with their good wishes, but their encouragement has grown more sincere with time. While they may never fail to suggest alternative careers, professions, and odd trades, I will always appreciate their insistence on imagining the best future for the people they love.

Foreword: Hope Arising from Despair

Elias Khoury

Saadallah Wannous died on May 15, 1997, the anniversary of the Nakba. From his deathbed, the playwright narrated the defeats and disasters of our time while his friend Omar Amiralay filmed him. Was it merely a coincidence, or did Wannous want his death to be the logical end to *There are So Many Things Still to Say* (1997), his film with the late director Amiralay? Did the author of the play *Soirée for the 5th of June* (1968) want the memory of the Nakba to fill the final chapter of his life before death?

Omar Amiralay died on February 5, 2011, before he could see the beginnings of the Syrian revolution. Still, his film *A Flood in Baath Country* (2003) testifies to the fall of the regime before its collapse. A twist of fate did not allow the narrator of *Drunken Days* (1997), Wannous's play based on a family story told to him by Amiralay, to see how the Syrian people would shatter the walls of their enormous prison in March 2011. When I thought about the significance of Wannous and the meaning of his texts about hope, I saw before me Omar Amiralay standing behind the camera, recording the image of his moribund playwright friend reflected in the drops of an intravenous line, hooked into the arteries of a man living his life in death.

With Omar's image, I remembered Abdul Rahman Munif, the late Saudi-Iraqi-Jordanian-Damascene writer who did not shy away from pronouncing the death of the *Cities of Salt* (1984–89). He was among the first to herald the fall of oppressive regimes with the publication of his novel *East of the Mediterranean*, first in 1975 and again in 1991 with the revised title *Here and Now … or East of the Mediterranean Again*, in which political prisons began to signify the beginning of the end of the mad oppressive regimes that occupied the Arab world. These three intellectuals in addition to a number of other writers, artists, freedom fighters, and prisoners of conscience founded a new culture, one which only fully emerged with today's generation of Syrian men and women who are bringing about a revolution from the heart of oppression and despair.

Saadallah Wannous was the most despondent of them all. He reached into the depths of despair searching for hope. He bore dejection and courage, and his eyes flashed like spotlights that refused to go black. His work spoke to the Arab peoples, breaking taboos and addressing their tragedies, ongoing since the great Palestinian Nakba.

In 1968, Wannous published his theatrical manifesto on the 1967 defeat, the play *Soirée for the 5th of June*, which contends that the defeat was the result of oppression and dictatorship. In 1977, he wrote *The King is King* when no one else in Syria dared to say to the dictator that the oppressor, *The Elephant, the King of All Time* (1969), was destroying the country. In 1990, he wrote the Nakba into his play *Rape*, a major cultural lesson rooted in his empathy with Palestine's trauma that broke down the barrier to broaching the subject of Israel: he was able, for the first time in the history of Arab theatre, to present multifaceted Israeli characters on the stage. In 1994, he wrote his magnum opus *Ritual for a Metamorphosis*. Wannous's ability to reconcile layers of narrative with the dramaturgical devices of epic theatre enabled him to explore the human experience at the core of social struggle.

And yet there remain those who claim that the Arab revolutions came out of nowhere, that they are a spontaneous social eruption!

When we went to Husayn Al Bahr just north of Tartous, Syria, to bury Saadallah Wannous in his final resting place beneath pregnant branches of olive trees, I was struck by Osama Mohammad. Mohammad had directed the film *Stars in Broad Daylight* (1988), a tour de force of culture in defiance of dictatorship. He had in his hands a poster with a picture of Saadallah and spoke about the courage of the young people who managed to print it. Osama said that in Syria, which the regime defined as "Assad's Syria," it was impossible to find a printer who would run a picture other than that of the president. He said that Saadallah Wannous achieved his final victory over the tyrant on the day of his burial.

We whispered. The village was nearly swallowed by the smoke belching from a nearby cement plant. We stood before a huge bronze statue of Hafez Al Assad elsewhere in the village, his hands open as if to embrace the beautiful Syrian coast, attempting, along with the smoke from the factory, to smother the seaside villages under the dust of oppression, its language fraught with fear, suspicion, and pretense.

Saadallah Wannous died 14 years before the great Syrian eruption, but of all the Syrian writers, he has been the most present since the outbreak of the revolution.

He has been a beacon not only because he authored the difficult beginnings but also because his words carry both the fervor and the great despair of the future. His sorrow signified the hope he forced upon himself and, in turn, his country.

* * *

I remember when I found the actors and actresses backstage at Beirut Theatre in their black clothes and Israeli costumes, chanting in the name of Arabism and Gamal Abdel Nasser, moments before going onstage. This is how these actors and actresses prepared to get into their Israeli characters in the production of *Rape* under Jawad Al Asadi's direction. The play was officially banned in Damascus, so it was performed in a private residence far from the eyes of the censors. When it toured cities in the Arab world, audiences were more than delighted. The actors – Dalaa Al Rahbi, Fayez Qazaq, and Ghassan Massoud – were excellent, and Jawad Al Asadi's direction was Artaudian in its cruelty.

But what truly struck a chord with audiences was, above all, Wannous's dialogue, a smooth mix of slang and simplified literary Arabic, free of stiff formalities. They were also taken by how the play dared to stage complex dialogues with the Other, the Israeli characters. By humanizing the characters, Wannous broke the barrier of fear, inhabiting through art a new approach to the resistance against the Israeli occupation at a time when political rhetoric had failed to do so.

However, not only did the director drop the Palestinian narrative from the play, but he also changed the ending, which was reason enough for Wannous to refuse to acknowledge the piece as his own. Despite Wannous's frustrations, even a fraction of the play as staged by Al Asadi sufficed to unleash creative flashes of lightning in the small Beirut Theatre.

When I visited Wannous in his home in the Birzeh neighborhood of Damascus and told him the story, I was surprised by the sadness that clouded his demeanor. I already knew that the playwright disagreed with how the director had synthesized *Rape*, but I wanted to tell him that half a good play suffices and that great art accommodates numerous readings.

I was not surprised by the man's sadness, for Saadallah Wannous was always sad, as if sorrow were his twin. Words ran from his fingers like water, an endless stream that never ceased to rush but could never quench his thirst. When he was stricken with cancer, Wannous was overtaken by a writing fever. Ink sprung from the depths of his soul, and the man himself became merely a conduit for his stories to emerge from the darkness of silence. Saadallah Wannous knew that he was headed towards the dark silence of the dead. He wanted to salvage his words from darkness, to bring his imagined characters to light through pools of ink.

* * *

I once asked Wannous about his use of literary Arabic, which, in his work, resembles colloquial speech in its simplicity. Through the course of our discussion about language, he told me that he began writing dialogue in colloquial dialect and then translated it to literary Arabic. I was and remain biased towards the usage of colloquial Arabic in plays and novels, but I was amazed by how Wannous overcame the sense of distance inherent to literary Arabic and managed to write in a language that encompassed the depths of the human experience, where all languages converge, their differences effaced.

Wannous had shared his secret. On that day, I understood that his attempts to subdue literary Arabic, perhaps the final such endeavor, were an effort to shape it for speech – lucid and pulsating with vitality. The logic that drove his language schemes was far more complicated than a mere nationalist bias towards literary Arabic. Even though I was not won over by his argument, I never cease to be dazzled by the ease with which Wannous fine-tuned literary Arabic for the stage.

Language was not the man's only secret. It was also a secret how Wannous raised difficult questions in the era of defeat and dictatorship. As his sense of loneliness deepened, he remained surrounded by the dozens of characters begotten by Wannous. His characters at once bore witness to and challenged the tides of Arab history.

I told him that half of *Rape* suffices, and I was not trying to appease him. It does suffice that we see Israeli characters in all their contradictions, and it suffices that we see how the occupier not only rapes his enemy but eventually also his fellow Israelis. It suffices that we read the final conversation between Wannous and Dr. Manuhin to discover that the door to our shared humanity, sealed shut by bitterness and hatred, can be opened by literature and actualized by theatre.

Soirée for the 5th of June, with its criticism of the self and its ascription of defeat to the tyranny afflicting the Arab world, found its other half in *Rape*. The latter play reaches into the depths of Palestine's trauma and interprets resistance as a framework through which Palestinians build their lives amidst the ruins of their homeland, amidst violence, amidst a brutal occupation.

* * *

Saadallah Wannous had only two things to say to *The King*: that the emperor has no clothes and that absolute power preys on people and kings alike. In true Brechtian form, the play told the dictator that he was nothing more than a role to fill on stage; it revealed how naked he truly was despite the masquerade of rhetoric.

Words envelope, words denude, and Wannous chose bare words to strip down power, to reveal societal paradoxes, and to raise difficult questions. Indeed, no other writer questioned so relentlessly. If the Arab revolutions stem from questions of culture and politics, then the body of work penned by Wannous, long before the outbreak of uprisings, forms the intellectual roots of the Syrian revolution.

Tyranny and authoritarianism have born nothing but deserts of words turned to sand. In these vast, harrowing deserts, Syrian writers and thinkers have created oases of freedom. They have dug deep to find wellsprings of language, and along its streams, they have planted the possibilities of the future. *Ritual for a Metamorphosis* emerged from the heart of these possibilities. In the play, Wannous deploys Brechtian devices to construct a multifaceted narrative about Damascus society. Desire erupts, frameworks collapse, stories soar in a limitless space, and theatre embraces life.

* * *

It is in Syria that the Arabs have taken themselves most by surprise. There, a new generation of freedom fighters has forged its relationship with life through resistance against despotism. Their creativity has transcended the conventional boundaries of protest, which will serve as an important lesson in sacrifice and victory for the sake of dignity, and Syrians have successfully transformed their demonstrations into weddings of freedom, with popular music, song, chanting, and dance. Cellphone cameras have transformed into tools of documentary. New forms of art using video, technology, theatre, puppetry, cinema, and writing have emerged.

A society was born on the brink of death, hope arose from despair, art was wrought by people's blood, pain, and cries that filled the sky. The Barada River runs red with blood, Ibrahim Al Qashoush[1] chants, Ali Ferzat's fingers[2] break as the regime tries to prevent his caricatures from rallying calls to resistance, playwrights are arrested but not silenced, filmmakers turn the camera into a mirror of freedom, and unarmed people have rendered barricades out of their chests and voices.

Translated by Meris Lutz

Notes

1. Ibrahim Al Qashoush (d. 2011) was a fireman, poet, and lyricist from Hama, a flashpoint city in the Syrian uprising. Hundreds of thousands of protestors sang his chants during the uprisings in Hama in June 2011. In early July, Qashoush disappeared. His body, with vocal chords slain, was found in the Orontes River on July 4, 2011.
2. Ali Ferzat (b. 1951) is the most prominent cartoonist in Syria and the broader Arab world, known for his satirical work that criticizes local politics, economy, and society. In August 2011, masked gunmen assaulted Ferzat, beat him, broke his hands, and dumped him on the side of the airport road in Damascus.

List of Plates

Plates are bound between pages 96 and 97

1

Introduction

Eyad Houssami

Writing about theatre fuels the process of making theatre. It is the drama critic and cultural historian whom society entrusts to capture what happens when audiences bear witness to performance. The critic, the scholar, the researcher – we rely on them to perceive action unfolding on the stage, to apprehend moments of horror and joy, to question why performance matters, and to register the slivers of truth that flash and restore our humanity.

Likewise, the playwright, actor, designer, dramaturg, or director who reflects on her work through writing not only strengthens her artistry through introspection and self-questioning, but she also inscribes her creative process onto the genealogy of theatre history. Indeed, to record the mundanity and profundity of artistic endeavors is to affirm our ability to imagine, propose, and inhabit alternative realities together through performance. Anecdotes about the invincibility and vulnerability that actors explore in rehearsal, stories about the bizarre and beautiful intimacy shared by strangers in the theatre – these accounts attest to how artists dare to tread unknown ontological frontiers. They document how making theatre is an endless experiment – of exploring what it means to be present, of enacting new ways of living together in the present, of transforming the givens of daily life, of remembering how to live.

These insights immortalize theatrical experience. They survive and often remain the most precious trace of performance, an inescapably ephemeral art bound by the exclusivity of the present. These accounts lift theatre from its fleeting moment and resurrect it in the imaginations of readers in another time and another place. Thus, through theatre writing, performance embarks on a journey that swiftly transcends borders and languages.

This book is a collection of essays on contemporary theatre and performance with a focus on the Arab stage. The writings revolve around the legacy of Saadallah Wannous, the late Syrian dramatist whose plays about tyranny resonate with audiences worldwide. Authored by playwrights, directors, and scholars in Arabic and English, these essays and accounts trace the reverberations of Wannous's repertoire in the Arab Middle East and beyond. The book brings together literary analyses of drama, histories of theatrical production, and narratives about making and teaching plays. In that regard, *Doomed by Hope: Essays on Arab Theatre* testifies to the singular force of playwriting, an artistic and literary craft that chronicles history, orchestrates dialogue, and forges culture.

It is my hope, as steward of the essays in this volume, that this book enables directors in Baghdad to glimpse into the theatre classroom of Birzeit University; that it allows actors in Port Said to envisage rehearsal in Kuwait; that it prompts playwrights in Tunis to consider the differences between theatre research in New York, Cairo, and Damascus; that it invites audiences to think more critically and deeply about theatre. Above all, the purpose of this book is to impart the knowledge and experiences of artists and scholars to those who have the desire to make and explore theatre but lack interlocutors.

The obstacles facing theatre practitioners in oligarchical and authoritarian Arab societies are daunting. In addition to the global onslaught of consumerism and proliferation of screens, decades of occupation by foreign forces and oppressive regimes have stifled culture and education, to say nothing of science and industry. Endemic corruption has rendered public speech void of meaning. Public discourse, so glutted with propaganda, has corroded the Arabic language itself, and the endless brain drain continues to drive highly literate and learned citizens into the diaspora. Nonetheless, and seemingly against all odds, theatre endures.

I first set out to make this book in 2008 when I was living in Damascus. The project emerged from a series of living room conversations with Dr. Marie Elias, a theatre scholar and translator who worked closely with Wannous. At the time, I was reading his plays and theatre writings and came across the address "Thirst for Dialogue," which he authored in 1996 for World Theatre Day, created by the International Theatre Institute, an affiliate of UNESCO.

Born in 1941 in a village north of Tartous, Syria, Wannous trained as a journalist in Cairo before devoting his life to theatre as a playwright, editor, administrator, and educator in Damascus. He authored 14 plays, penned dozens of theatre writings, established and edited the journal *Hayat Al Masrah* (Life of Theatre), and participated in the founding of the High Institute of Dramatic Arts in Damascus in the late 1970s, one of the only theatre conservatories in the entire Arab Middle East.

"Thirst for Dialogue" is among the last texts he wrote before he died of cancer in 1997. In the address, Wannous deplores the paradoxes of global capital and the technological revolution. Despite extraordinary wealth and greater interconnectivity, economic inequality increases, culture withers, society fragments, and the isolation of the individual grows deeper. The "global village" utopia is in fact a dystopia that has endangered theatre. Wannous laments that theatre has never before suffered from such neglect, such a lack of moral and financial support.

He draws parallels between "self-serving globalization," void of any trace of humanity, and the cancer infesting his body. He cites playwriting as "the most significant means of [his] resistance" against the disease. Playwriting prolongs life, and through his dying days, Wannous persists. Writing for theatre acquires existential meaning, perhaps even biological utility. Despite his acknowledgment that theatre was and remains "under siege [by the forces of neoliberalism] and on the verge of vanishing from our lives," Wannous does not waver:

> I insist on writing for the theatre because I want to defend it. I struggle so that this vital art will go on living ... Theatre is in fact more than art. It is a complex civilizational phenomenon. If we lose and deprive ourselves of theatre, the world will become a more forlorn, ugly, and impoverished place.[1]

His prophecy may be grim, but Wannous concludes his address on a note of optimism, "convinced" that goodwill shall prevail and protect culture, and that, in turn, theatre will return to its rightful place: "We are doomed by hope, and come what may, today cannot be the end of history."

That phrase, "doomed by hope," occurs as a refrain in his address. It resonated with Wannous's public and to this day holds remarkable currency in Arab culture, certainly in theatre. In "Thirst for Dialogue" and his repertoire more broadly, Wannous renders hope a paradoxical force: as it kindles our faith in the promise of the future, it propels humanity towards the oblivion of death. Evoking the image of a cancer-stricken man, "doomed by hope" also conveys the Sisyphean nature of making theatre in societies ruled by totalitarian or oligarchical regimes that stifle and punish artists who dare to challenge the prescriptions for cultural expression. Come what may, we are condemned to defend theatre.

* * *

When I was studying and practicing theatre as an undergraduate at Yale, I sensed the dire need for what this book has become. When, a decade after Wannous's passing, I moved to Damascus and then to Beirut, my experiences as a theatre artist, critic, and researcher affirmed the book's urgency. When revolts and uprisings began to unfurl across the Arab Middle East in late 2010, I couldn't help myself: I had to bring the idea to fruition.

In the book's inception, I turned to the very scholars, critics, and historians whose theatre writings had first lured me to the Arab Middle East: Nehad Selaiha, Marvin Carlson, and Marie Elias. Revered, widely published, and endlessly knowledgeable, they lent their expertise to the project by helping to shape its conceptual foundations. I sought support from the Prince Claus Fund for Culture and Development[2] and, with the Fund as a partner, launched the call for papers in Arabic and English on March 15, 2011, the day often described as the start of nationwide revolts against the Assad regime in Syria.

We sought original contributions in both languages from academics and artists and invited submissions – critical though not necessarily academic – that investigated the central themes and questions of Wannous's "Thirst for Dialogue," particularly in theatre and performance from the Arab Middle East. We encouraged writers to draw on their personal experience, reflecting deeply on a life in the theatre.

Many, if not most, books about Arab theatre and culture maintain the wide lens of a regional or national survey. They obscure the nuances that characterize the multitude of societies in the Middle East and the diaspora in order to draw sweeping, essentializing conclusions about a land mass, a religion, a language, or 300 million people. Moreover, rarely do artists themselves author the narratives, analyses, or research that form the central pillars of cultural historiography. Scholars, ensconced in universities, steer the discourse, which privileges theoretical approaches reliant on already published and archival material at the expense of experiential accounts, which almost never materialize in print. By seeking the insights of practitioners in addition to the invaluable perspectives of researchers, *Doomed by Hope* aims to bridge the gap between the academy and the stage in theatre historiography, as actor Hanane Hajj Ali did in her notable book, *Theatre Beyrouth*.[3]

Moreover, we wished to complicate and deepen the discourse by grounding the book in questions, at once historically specific and intellectually abstract, in an effort to unsettle the parameters that usually bound writing about culture in Arabic and English. Notions of origin, authenticity, censorship, nationhood, postcolonialism, Islam, and dissent frame and saturate discussions about culture, usually assessed and interpreted in terms of its political cunning to the exclusion of its aesthetic, poetic, philosophical, and psycho-emotional qualities. We strived to coalesce these various approaches to interpreting art by asking contributors to probe if and how theatre "will remain the ideal place where man can reflect upon both his historical and existential condition," as Wannous said in his address.

We received a total of 40 submissions and proposals in Arabic and English. Due to the exigencies of the political situation, a number of prolific and innovative theatre makers could not participate. Some directors and playwrights in Tunisia and Syria, for instance, were pivotal to revolt, social movement, and uprising. The extraordinary urgency and tremendous demands of activism left little time for writing. Those who did respond to the call for papers hailed from Morocco to Saudi Arabia to New Zealand as well as countries engrossed by protest, and the submissions ran the gamut from descriptive chronologies of national theatre histories, teeming with lists and genealogies, to personal memoirs.

The texts were reviewed by the core editorial committee – Drs. Selaiha, Carlson, and Elias – and a number of external Arabic and English readers outside the field. I was determined to see a book like this come to fruition in both English and Arabic, as opposed to only Arabic, because I believed that the editorial and rhetorical practices of the two languages would enrich the project with a singular diversity and would reflect divergent ways of thinking about – and therefore making – theatre. There is a dire need for cross-pollination and exchange between Anglophone and Arabophone theatre. Translation of dramatic literature and theatre scholarship between the two languages is tragically minimal. Each theatre culture needs and benefits from translation. After all, theatre is inherently multilingual, embracing as it does stories and characters from myriad acts of human history.

* * *

The histories, analyses, and narratives in *Doomed by Hope* focus on the process of contemporary theatre practice. Together, with an arresting foreword by novelist Elias Khoury, the essays zoom into definitive moments of Saadallah Wannous's life and repertoire, and they illuminate how Wannous's legacy manifests itself in and informs theatre today – from reading plays in a classroom and writing plays for a city to performing in a security state and directing in theatres, prisons, and international festivals in a time of revolt.

The photography, by Dalia Khamissy, Yazan Khalili, and Joseph Seif, consolidates these elements of the book. The series of portraits and photographs of venues and universities not only serve to flesh out the settings and characters that populate the pages of this book, but the photography also culls together the various spaces in which contemporary theatre develops and happens: the stage, laptop screen, kitchen table, home, backstage, conservatory, neighborhood, art school, and university. Through photography, we were also able to include artists like playwright Mohammad Attar, actor Fadi Abi Samra, directors Oussama Ghanem and Issam Boukhaled, and the performers of Collectif Kahraba, as well as venues such as the Egyptian National Theatre in Cairo's Attaba Square and Beirut Theatre in the Lebanese capital. While these artists and settings do not necessarily illustrate a particular essay in the book, they engage directly with the themes and questions of *Doomed by Hope*, and they stand at the forefront of the struggle to defend theatre, as Wannous put it.

In the first two essays of *Doomed by Hope*, scholars Edward Ziter and Rania Jawad analyze plays by Wannous and shed light on how his theatre dislodges the structures of tyranny, from the mid twentieth century until today. Ziter, a professor of drama at New York University (NYU), situates Wannous's seminal play, *Soirée for the 5th of June* (1968), in the wake of Syria's stupefying defeat in the 1967 War with Israel, a catastrophe that few intellectuals and artists dared to address critically. As it attributes defeat to the paralyzing practices of totalitarianism, *Soirée* overturns the hierarchy of state-sanctioned theatrical representation, subsequently enabling the audience to defy the state and to forge a national identity, as Ziter maintains.

Rania Jawad writes about teaching Wannous in Birzeit University as revolts unfurl across the Arab Middle East. A PhD candidate at NYU, Jawad sheds light on the links between theatre and the performances of power acted out in Israel-Palestine. Her essay parses student readings of Wannous and pedagogical techniques in Palestine before shifting the focus to theatre practice in a West Bank refugee camp.

The essays by Dalia Basiouny and Samia Habib about theatre in Egypt investigate the construction of collective memory in a time of revolt. Basiouny, a theatre artist and drama teacher at the American University in Cairo, discusses the creative and production process of her documentary theatre performance, *Tahrir Stories*, presented in Cairo as the Egyptian revolution was erupting. Habib, a cultural critic, offers a glimpse of theatrical activity on a national level in the spring following the ouster of former president Hosni Mubarak.

From the vantage point of university professors and scholars, Katherine Hennessey, Asaad Al-Saleh, and Meisoun Ali explore theatre in Yemen and Syria in the years leading up to the 2011 revolts. Hennessey hones in on three performances in 2009 and 2010 in Yemen, arguing that theatre presaged how, just a couple of years later, youth protestors would enact their desires for social and political change in public spaces. Al-Saleh and Ali ground their contributions in playwriting in Syria from Wannous to the years leading up to the present. Assistant professor of literature and cultural studies at the University of Utah, Al-Saleh anchors his academic essay, like Ziter, in *Soirée for the 5th of June* but offers an alternative reading of Wannous's theatre.

He highlights the function of dialogue in *Soirée* and other plays while also referring to literary and cultural scholarship published in Arabic. Ali, a professor at the High Institute of Dramatic Arts in Damascus, foregrounds the voices of the new generation of Syrian writers in order to raise questions about the trajectory of playwriting.

Theatre makers Abdullah Al Kafri, Zeina Daccache, Rabih Mroué, and Sulayman Al Bassam offer narrative accounts and searing insights into contemporary theatre practice in Syria, Lebanon, Kuwait, and on the international circuit. Playwright Al Kafri unravels the nexus of administration and craft by showing how an independent theatre scene in Damascus bypasses the ossified cultural apparatuses of the state to engage in theatrical artistry. The essays by Al Kafri, Meisoun Ali, and Samia Habib are edited versions based on translations by Meris Lutz.

Daccache and Mroué, both acclaimed theatre makers based in Lebanon, investigate performance that reconfigures legal paradigms. Daccache reflects on her experience as a drama therapist and theatre director in Roumieh Prison, working with a group of actors to develop an adaptation of Reginald Rose's play *Twelve Angry Men*. Grounding his essay in questions raised by *Rape* (1990) by Wannous, multidisciplinary artist Mroué plunges into a line of inquiry about performance in the security state. Seasoned theatre director Al Bassam looks back on nearly a decade of staging adaptations of Shakespeare in Arabic and of working transnationally in the Arab Middle East and producing work internationally. Al Bassam departs from the legacy of Wannous and advocates a political theatre addressing international audiences.

Joseph Shahadi and Margaret Litvin turn to performance in diaspora and in festivals while drawing attention to the nuances of cultural production linked to the Arab Middle East in the United States. An artist and performance studies scholar, Shahadi dissects a one-woman show by Jennifer Jajeh to argue that stagings of Palestinian national identity may occur in diasporic contexts. Litvin, a professor at Boston University and author of the book *Hamlet's*

Arab Journey (2011), examines two major cultural festivals in Washington, DC, and New York in 2009, contending that the American market for Arab theatre is a positive development.

Finally, in a poetic and intimate personal essay, Jawad Al Asadi evokes his memories of collaborating with Wannous. The renowned Iraqi theatre director and playwright plunges into the past and Wannous's repertoire and concludes the book in a requiem to the late dramatist and his legacy. "Wannous knew how to defeat death. He knew how to teach death a lesson," Al Asadi writes. "Perhaps Wannous's greatest achievement was writing texts that affirm life in the face of death. Writing bounded him to existence."

Notes

1. Saadallah Wannous, "al-Jou ila al-Hiwar" [Thirst for Dialogue], in *al-Aamal al-Kamilah* [The Complete Works] (Beirut: Dar Al Adab, 2004), 1:39–44. Translation by the editor.
2. Established in 1996, the Prince Claus Fund is based in Amsterdam and supported by the Dutch Ministry of Foreign Affairs and the Dutch Postcode Lottery. The organization views culture as a basic need and pursues cultural collaborations "where resources and opportunities for cultural expression, creative production, and research are limited and [where] cultural heritage is threatened," as stated on the Fund's website, accessed March 4, 2012, www.princeclausfund.org/en/the-fund.
3. Hanane Hajj Ali, *Theatre Beyrouth* [Beirut Theatre] (Beirut: Amers Editions, 2010). The book has been published in Arabic only.

2

Refugees on the Syrian Stage: *Soirée for the 5th of June*

Edward Ziter

In the aftermath of the 1967 War, *Soirée for the 5th of June*[1] (1968) by Saadallah Wannous was the only Syrian play to directly address its nation's defeat by the Israelis. Beyond the simple audacity of discussing such a sensitive subject, the play is remarkable for its insistence that the event be taken as an opportunity to define a Syrian identity in defiance of a state that had rendered its population deaf and dumb. The play openly asserts that Syrians are saddled with a false and incomplete identity because their government has denied them free speech, and that this persecution resulted in defeat in the 1967 War. What is much less transparent, however, are the strategies through which Wannous attempts to induce his audience into such a controversial self-imagining.

The process, I will argue, entails two interrelated steps, both of which reverse the hierarchy of representation. First, Wannous invents a site of free exchange where none exists by imagining a theatre in which audience members are fully empowered to reject the planned bill of fare and substitute questioning, debate, and their own spontaneous performances. Second, Wannous stages this revolutionary theatre through interventions of the voiceless. The refugee – the figure whose presence and representation are objects of considerable control and concern throughout the Arab world –

upends the performance when he innocently notes the difference between his experience of flight and that represented in the official culture of state theatre.

Thus, *Soirée for the 5th of June* transforms the carefully stage-managed visibility of the refugee into unmanageable speech. Unconscious of the revolutionary nature of his action, the token refugee rises from his seat with other invited guests and claims the stage. In this moment, the play embarks on a project of redrawing the boundaries of Syrian identity by forcing the audience to fully engage that figure who manifests the fragility of national boundaries. Wannous asks his audience to find common cause with the refugees of the Golan Heights by asserting that all in the audience have been expatriated from a proper understanding of self by a government that has colonized its people's psyches.

Before taking up this remarkable play, some contextualization is in order. Only a few Syrian playwrights have dared to interrogate Syria's military conflicts with Israel. As noted, Wannous's play is unique in directly examining the 1967 War; however, other plays have addressed the war indirectly. Mamdouh Udwan's *The Trial of the Man Who Didn't Fight* (1971), which is set during the thirteenth-century invasion of Iraq and Syria by the Mongul leader Hulagu Khan, examines territorial loss and culpability. While the play makes no mention of 1967, it clearly resonates with the war four years prior. Ali Aqla Arsan's *The Palestinian Women* (1971) depicts a group of Palestinians caught in the confusion of the 1948 War and then some 18 years later in a refugee camp – the 1967 War looms on the outer edge of the play. As such, the play presents Palestinian disenfranchisement as a precursor to a catastrophe that the audience does not witness but knows is about to occur. In *The Jester* (1973), Muhammad Al Maghut depicts a Syrian state that is indifferent to territorial loss, despite the ubiquity of liberation rhetoric. In that irreverent play, the Andalusian conqueror Abd Al Rahman I has returned from the dead to reclaim Palestine, only to be detained at the Syrian-Israeli border by Syrian officials who extradite him to Spain for medieval war crimes in return for a shipment of Spanish onions. These four plays stand out in the history of Syrian theatre for examining Arab defeat at a time when most attempts in other media to explore the Syrian psyche after 1967 – particularly media involving a mass audience – did not see the light of day.

Several plays written immediately after the 1973 War embrace the enthusiasm of the moment. Ali Aqla Arsan's *The Strangers* (1974) depicts a small village that allows a group of strangers to encamp, only to find that the strangers evict residents from portions of the village and eventually take over the village square. Scattered references to the 1948 War make the analogy clear: the village is the Arab world, and the square is Palestine. Only after the mayor rallies the entire village do they successfully stand up against the strangers. While the extent of their victory is not indicated, it is clear that the villagers have redeemed themselves. Mustafa Al Hallaj's *Hey Israeli, It's Time to Surrender* (1974) similarly describes Arab redemption. A young peasant woman risks her life and that of her infant to capture an armed Israeli pilot whose plane has been shot down in the war. In Hallaj's play, a woman manifests a people's honor and demonstrates that Arabs will stand their ground.

Muhammad Al Maghut's *October Village* (1974) both engages the post-1973 War enthusiasm and subtly critiques it by noting the cost at which this partial victory came. In this play, the theft of a groom's vineyard delays a marriage for decades despite the promises of a series of village leaders to reclaim the lost land. At the play's close, it is revealed that the men of the village have set off in secrecy against the thieves; they return victorious, but the play's comic hero has died in battle. The sorrow amidst celebration further complicates what is already a strangely sudden change in tone. The play is a relentless, cynical black comedy about the perfidy of Arab leaders, so it feels ironic when the actors turn to the audience at the close of the play to announce that every Arab nation supports their project of liberating the Golan, Sinai, and occupied Jordan (i.e. the West Bank).

Syria's actions during the 1982 Lebanon War are a particularly sensitive subject, and it is not surprising that Saadallah Wannous was the only Syrian playwright to address this in *Historical Miniatures* (1994). That play depicts the futile resistance of a handful of Damascenes to Tamerlane's invasion circa 1400. Characters in the play condemn the Sultan for his failure to "guide the nation in its need" or "safeguard its land and its people." However, the real object of the play's critique is revealed when a character recounts a dream that foreshadows the Israeli's invasion of Beirut. In the dream, she finds herself in Beirut as iron birds roar overhead, tossing down "fiery horrible balls that echo and annihilate." Her dream culminates as she notices that all around Arabs representing the many nations of the Arab world watch "without concern," an indictment of all of the present-day Arab sultans.[2] It is also worth noting the courageousness of Wannous's play *Rape*, which is unique in the Syrian cannon in presenting both Palestinians and Israelis as victims of the Israeli security apparatus. Only one other Syrian play approaches *Rape* in its psychologically complex depictions of Palestinians and Israelis: Mamdouh Udwan's *If You Were Palestinian* (1981), which depicts (among other things) a Palestinian splinter group that takes an Israeli archeologist, his aide, and his niece hostage.

Soirée for the 5th of June is structured around an elaborate theatrical conceit; the audience has supposedly come to the theatre to see an entirely different play, *The Murmur of Ghosts*. This fiction is introduced soon after the curtain rises. After an initially unexplained delay, an actor playing the embarrassed director of *The Murmur of Ghosts* steps forward to apologize for assembling an audience despite the fact that the play cannot be performed, but the tickets had already been issued and a number of guests invited. No mention is made of the actual advertised play, *Soirée for the 5th of June*, or its playwright, Saadallah Wannous. Instead, this director explains why he felt it was important to commission a play on the recent war, a play entitled *The Murmur of Ghosts*, written by "Abd Al Ghani." No one in the audience has ever heard of Abd Al Ghani, but he is supposedly a well-known playwright and the author of this evening's entertainment.

The "director" begins to recount his initial conversations with Abd Al Ghani with an actor from the troupe playing the supposed playwright when suddenly the "real" Abd Al Ghani emerges from the audience and offers to play himself. Their conversation about a potential play is illustrated by the troupe, which performs scenes from *The Murmur of Ghosts*, the inexplicably unperformable play. As the summary/dramatization is relatively brief, the director explains that the troupe will now entertain the audience with folk dances. It is at this point that a refugee from the Golan interrupts the proceedings with questions that send the show in a very different direction.

From the outset, Wannous establishes that this audience will speak, and this willingness to talk back to the stage is essential to his project of transforming the performance into a rehearsal for civil society. Actors in the audience play the part of impatient audience members, complaining about the delay. We get a hint of this "audience's" potential for political speech when one of these false spectators complains that the delay reflects a "contempt for the audience," prompting another to quip "or it's an imperialist plot" (25). The two statements resonate rather than clash with each other, for the ascription of all failures to ubiquitous imperialism evidences far more contempt than mere delays. The joke implies a jaded cynicism in the face of official culture, whether it is explanations for holding the curtain at the National Theatre or excuses for failures on the battlefield.

This "audience" shifts from cynical interjections to angry condemnation after the director presents his theatrical vision of the night when hostilities broke out: chaos and confusion as experienced from the vantage point of a child. By focusing on the child's experience, the director effectively casts the Syrian people as a naïve and pacifist population, ignorant of the issues that underlie the conflict and incapable of undertaking the management and defense of the nation. However, audience members reject such a representation: "But that's a fairytale! You and your silent confused characters are a joke. Your child is a rag doll." Ignoring other audience members who advise him not to overstep his place, the spectator continues: "Our war is an old and just hope. We all remember that morning. The streets were full of people. We embraced each other. We cried with excitement and enthusiasm" (39–40). The defiance of this audience member prompts a rush of memories from other supposed audience members.

> Spectator 1: By God, that's right.
> Spectator 2: The women in our neighborhood trilled till their voices became hoarse.
> Spectator 3: What do you want? That's how war breaks out in American movies. (40)

If there is an imperialist plot, it lies in the cultural imperialism that infects even the tropes through which official culture imposes a depoliticized image of the people onto the nation.

The stage, and particularly the national stage where this production was mounted, is far removed from the coffee shop in which (arguably) the people are permitted to speak. In effect, Wannous is attempting to transform the theatre into a coffee shop and then to make the coffee shop a space in which people feel empowered to discuss politics.[3] In addition to denying the audience a right to speak, the director denies that he, as an artist, is confined by fact. The director's argument begins innocuously when he prefaces his entertainment by explaining that "memory is not the specialty of the theatre but rather the specialty of the historian"; the only specialty of the theatre is "art" (27). From this vantage point, he easily dismisses the contrasting memory of the audience, as well as their right to speak back to the stage. He states, "I don't understand the justification for these outbursts ... I wanted to present a theatrical vision of the start of the war, no more" (40). Through the director's haughty disregard of the facts, Wannous attempts to excite audience indignation at authority's monopoly over the representation of the past.

Wannous's actors/audience members are able to contest the director's vision of the beginning of the war, but they are forced to sit silently once the play shifts to depictions of the front. Their dilemma, the dilemma of Syrians in general, is that without access to the facts of their defeat, they have little ability to debate its immediate causes and significance. This is not to say that Wannous makes his audience passive consumers of official representations of the past (whether those representations are mounted on the national stage or narrated by the national news service). Instead, *The Murmur of Ghosts* prompts disbelief with its overblown rhetoric of resistance. The people of the Golan retreat, but they do so only to insure that the battle will continue. As one of the villagers explains, a "treacherous and powerful enemy" has taken the village by surprise, but retreat will "preserve [their] children and the wombs of [their] women," ensuring victory in some unspecified future (59). Meanwhile, a handful of peasant farmers stay on to fight, despite certain death. The ghosts of dead soldiers remain with them. These ghosts promise to cloud the minds of the invaders, fill their sleep with nightmares, and in doing so prevent any lasting Israeli settlement (67). The promise that ghosts would liberate the Golan was no less ridiculous in 1968 than it is today, and it served to spotlight the cynicism of a government whose official media could assert that the war had been a victory because it had not resulted in the overthrow of the Baath regime.[4]

At this point, we learn that Abd Al Ghani forbade performance of the play. No sooner had he completed the work than he began to fear that he had prostituted his talents, trotting out well-worn and cheaply pleasing lies such as a steadfast peasantry committed to national liberation. According to the playwright, his pages began to give off the "repulsive stench of a whore's crotch" (70) – implicitly casting any in the audience who delighted in images of Syrian heroism as clients in the market for tawdry delusions.

Disregarding the playwright's complaints, the director quickly moves on to the evening's replacement entertainment. Since the setting of *The Murmur of Ghosts* "recalls the old festivals," the troupe will use it as a backdrop for the performance of "rural songs and dances," placing "nostalgia and delight in the very place in which heroism was glorified" (71). The depiction of steadfast and nationalistic villagers in *The Murmur of Ghosts* has as much basis in fact as the director's troupe of happy peasants comfortably ensconced in their villages.

In lieu of history, the director offers nostalgia. His soirée is not an exploration of recent events but rather a presentation of fetishized imagery designed to soothe a troubled population: nationalistic villagers and the happy folk dancing and singing as they have done for countless centuries and will continue to do long into the future. As Freud explains, the fetish serves to mask an unsettling absence, one that strikes deeply at the essence of one's identity.[5] *Soirée for the 5th of June* explores the absence of a meaningful national identity, an absence evident in the ease with which Israelis swept Syrians from the Golan, an absence displaced through the fictionalized image of the resistant folk. As if invoking Freud, Abd Al Ghani describes the experience of looking beyond the fetishized villager as the shock of discovering sexual difference: he likens his play to a prostitute's genitalia. As in Freud's discussion of the fetish, discovering the absence of national identity is a trauma that can only be displaced through the substitution of a pleasing screen – steadfast villagers and folk dances.

Despite the director's efforts at displacement, the refugee takes over the evening's performance as an old man in faded trousers, dark blue jacket, and white kaffiyeh, who stands up to ask the name of that remarkable village depicted on stage (72). The contrast between this supposedly real refugee and the theatre's happy noble peasants arrests the celebration of Syrian heroism; the soirée becomes an examination of loss – not simply the loss of land but a preceding loss of self. From the opening stage directions of *Soirée for the*

5th of June, Wannous draws the reader's attention to the contradictory hierarchy of representations that greet spectators at an "official theatre" on opening night. There are the "traditional invitations for officials and the pillars of authority" as well as "the other traditional invitations for a number of refugees and citizens of the third estate" (23).

The choice to use an antiquated term, "third estate," rather than a more common – and deeply loaded – term like "the people" (*al shaab*), rings as an indictment of an atavistic society. Two hundred years earlier in France, political theorist Emmanuel Joseph Sieyes argued that the third estate attends to nineteen-twentieths of all public functions for the parasitic upper socio-economic orders. It would seem that Wannous saw a similar dynamic in "modern" Syrian society with the Baath Party and its supporters occupying the role formerly held by the nobility and clergy. However, lest one think such a theatre is isolated from current events, the stage directions further clarify that the refugees who have been invited are the product of "existing situations," which is to say that these are refugees from the Golan, and not from Palestine. The need for clarification implicitly asserts that the state has made a policy of manipulating the visibility of the refugee to serve state ends. As prominent members of the audience, they may be seen but not heard from.

This hierarchy is undermined when one of these invited refugees becomes the center of the audience's attention. What is the name of that remarkable village? The question draws attention to the obvious fact that the director's vision of recent events is fiction. The refugee, his son, and another companion approach the stage, posing questions and speaking among themselves as if the theatre were a town hall. They note the huge difference between the behavior of the people from his village and the stage's villagers: "How fine, how beautiful their organization is!" (75). The three then recount anecdotes that reveal an uneducated and unsophisticated rural population fleeing in confusion, driven by fear and greed rather than nationalism. Even more disturbing to the director's representations, the refugees encountered fleeing soldiers that were similarly naïve. Some fled the front in tears, ascribing superhuman powers to the Israelis. Others never saw any action but spent their time wasting what little ammunition they had shooting at bottles and tree stumps.

The audience is riveted by the refugees' tale even as it evokes horror and disgust. Spectators ask: "Why did you leave even before the war broke out?" (87), but the refugees, in their seclusion from the modern discourse of nationalism, do not even understand the question.[6] In this context, the audience rejects the director's repeated calls to begin the dancing. As one spectator exclaims:

> You and your dance troupe! For shame! Do you think that all we need is an hour of singing and dancing! You and your folk troupe can go to a country without problems. Settle there and provide the people with recreation. But here, we're a country with refugee camps. With people who left their village and don't know why. Listen to me ... the abscess is bleeding, and jesting won't stop abscesses from bleeding. (88)

Repeatedly, audience members describe not sympathy but revulsion at the sight of the refugees, like the sight of a bleeding abscess on the face of nationalism:

> If one village had resisted, it would have changed the meaning greatly. But before the war started, their inhabitants fled. They left behind land without people to the enemy, houses without people, cities without people. That also reflects a truth that has significance and a putrid stink like dirty armpits. (98)

The director had attempted to paper over this ugly absence, populating the empty houses of the Golan with valiant ghosts and hiding guerrilla fighters in the shadows of empty villages. However, the presence of (supposedly) real refugees on the national stage denudes this representation of pretense.

The refugee reveals the tenuous nature of national belonging, especially in nations that suppress forms of civic identification. Without mutually agreed-upon structures of social and political expression, the nation is nothing more than images of happy villagers and folk dances. *Soirée for the 5th of June* illustrates how easily such images are swept by the wayside in times of crisis. The theatre provides a setting that "recalls the old festivals"; the refugee describes a field of tents "that provide no protection from the heat or the cold" (86). The disjuncture between the two marks the distance between the myth of Syrian nationalism and the experience of dispossession that comes from living under authoritarianism.

The presence of the refugee produces a deep sense of "national abjection," to borrow cultural studies scholar Karen Shimakawa's evocative phrase. Following the lead of scholars such as Shimakawa and Maurice Stevens, it is useful to adapt psychoanalytic technique to understand collective trauma as a distinct social experience, rather than the aggregate of individual traumas.[7] Of particular value is their adaptation of philosopher Julia Kristeva's theories of psychosexual development for understanding structures of national belonging.

For Kristeva, the abject defines and recalls the moment in human development when an infant begins to become an individual by recognizing the mother to be separate from, rather than an extension of, the self. The abject resides at the boundary between self and other, threatening to undermine the idea of the individuated subject. As Kristeva says, "Abjection preserves what existed in the archaism of the pre-objectal relationship, in the immemorial violence with which a body becomes separated from another body in order to be – maintaining that night in which the outline of the signified thing vanishes and where only the imponderable affect is carried out."[8] A corpse produces the sensation of abjection, according to Kristeva, because it evokes that boundary at which an individual reverts to all-consuming materiality (the primordial Real in Lacan's terms). One responds in horror to the abject because of the persistent fear of dissolving back into that corroding night wherein "the outline of the signified thing vanishes."

In *Soirée for the 5th of June*, the refugee similarly stands on the border of national identification. As the figure without a home, he powerfully evokes the idea of the homeland through his negative example just as he illustrates the fragility of such ideas of belonging. It all can be swept away in a moment, and therein rests the horror. As sociologist Kai Erikson has documented, human-made catastrophes strike at a community's social bonds, producing the "gradual realization that the community no longer exists as an effective source of support and that an important part of the self has disappeared."[9] *Soirée for the 5th of June* depicts the wrenching of the social fabric as characters experience a profound isolation in realizing that the dictums of their society are false. If one village had resisted, the spectator complains, it would have changed the meaning greatly. Instead, we are left with "a bleeding abscess" and "a putrid stink like dirty armpits." The play forces its audience to stare into the face of the refugee, the national abject, and so contemplate the weak ties of Syrian national identity. The audience members' identities as national subjects are as shallow and false as the dancing and singing peasantry on the national stage.

Kristeva defines abjection as a precondition for self-recognition; similarly, the characters in *Soirée for the 5th of June* now begin the arduous process of identifying a Syrian self. In their discussions, audience members repeatedly ask who was responsible for the loss of the Golan and whether the audience members – as representatives of the nation – are themselves responsible. However, that question, according to one of the spectators, assumes that there is a "we" capable of taking responsibility. Having mounted the stage, this spectator draws an imaginary mirror and invites the audience to look upon themselves: "In order to bear responsibility, one needs to exist, and to have an image in the mirror. Well ... Do we exist?!" (103). Not finding an image, the spectator then asserts that the "national authority erased the image before it formed or became visible." In the play's most compelling and daring move, a group of spectators perform a drama of national erasure:

> Spectator 2: Don't speak. Tongues err. Words taste bitter. For the sake of the national authority, cut off your tongues.
> Spectator: (*from the hall*) Cutting off tongues would be benign.
> Spectator 2: And we cut off our tongues.
> Spectator 1: Why have we cut off our tongues?
> Spectator 2: Even if we haven't cut off our tongues, never forget the national interest: a prison of no sunlight, not even once a year. (115)

In this manner, the group of spectators acts out the process by which they cut out their tongues, cut off their ears, and cast aside their intellects. In the face of this oppressive state, the nation is prevented from creating a coherent image of itself, and the social imagination is left bereft.

The audience looks again into the imaginary mirror and sees only faint shadows behind the national authority – a game of backgammon, a water pipe, listening to popular songs. In short, the limited aspects of civil society permitted are informal, unstructured, and personal. These faint shadows of a nation, a spectator notes, dispersed like clouds by the winds of war (102).

Lacan famously defined the *mirror stage* as the period in subject formation during which the infant confronts a coherent external image of the self that exceeds the jumble of opposing drives and emotions experienced. At the level of national subject formation, *Soirée for the 5th of June* describes a people arrested in the development of a coherent self-image; the audience stares into the mirror but sees nothing beyond a jumble of shared experiences that dissipates before an image of the nation can come into focus, a jumble that vanishes in moments of crisis. How then to form a nation without full freedom of speech and assembly?

The answer, according to Wannous's play, would seem to lie in the powerful sense of hope and common cause that swept through Damascus when the Israeli invasion was announced. Audience members recount that streets and squares were overfilling with people, every window and door was open, people cried with enthusiasm, and there was a common belief that "a long period of shame would come to an end, justice and sovereignty would be established, and misery turned aside for ever" (114). This crowd included all members of society: itinerant peddlers, sellers of lottery tickets, even the desperately poor. The language of the audience members takes on a poetic quality as the discourse recalls a revolutionary sense of community. Audience members announce in sequence: the hungry had forgotten their hunger; the naked had forgotten their nakedness; the duped forgot their frauds; the persecuted forgot their persecution on that day in June (115). All had only one desire: to share in the defense of the homeland.

> Spectator 7: We were united in that succinct clear call.
> What do you ask for?
> The Group: Weapons. (116)

The shift in tense is significant. The audience remembers a past moment when collective action seemed possible; moreover, the memory politicizes the audience in the moment it is recounted. The demand for weapons is both past and present. Time in the play functions much as Walter Benjamin describes time for the ancient Jews: every second is the straight gate through which the messiah – or rather, the revolution – might enter.[10]

The scene depicts the birth of a true national consciousness, and like any birth it is not without danger. The director, an increasingly reactionary figure, accuses the audience of making his theatre the "seat of conspiracy."

According to the spectator who first drew the imaginary mirror on stage, this call for weapons marks the beginning of "our existence." Only now can the audience look into that mirror and perceive the outline of a nation: "our images are visible, images they call conspiracy." The statement prompts another spectator to respond, "Then terror spreads" (116). The concern is justified. If the people demand the right to defend the nation, they will necessarily challenge those who have labored to prevent the creation of institutions outside of direct governmental control and surveillance.

By 1968, successive Syrian governments had already demonstrated the lengths to which they would go to retain power. At first, though, audience members simply assert their desire to defend the homeland against foreign invaders. Bakers volunteer to stuff their bread with bombs for the invaders to consume; blacksmiths want to plant nails beneath the feet of the enemy; women wish to make bullets and bombs from their jewelry, to wear helmets instead of makeup, and to carry riffles rather than handbags (118). However, the idea of the national enemy shifts in the course of the scene. "It was our war," audience members repeatedly assert. However, the war is not simply against Israel but against usurpers and thieves, against the defenders of thieves, against hunger, misery, and daily death (119). Defense of the nation requires revolution.

Well before this point, security personnel had secured the exits, preventing any of the spectators from exiting. Now, one of the officials in the front row stands up, giving directions to the men guarding the doors to fan out. They surround the entire hall, take out their pistols, and point them at the audience, singling out those who took part in the discussion (121). As they purge the audience of troublemakers, the official delivers a triumphant speech that runs for several pages, celebrating the staying power of the state – a reprisal of the arguments made on national radio following the defeat. The audience's uprising has been a mere "infection" of the "infidel colonialist powers and their client states" (125). As the entire audience exits under guard, actors in the audience continue to comment on the evening and the failure of the larger audience to protect the more vocal spectators. Civil society will not come to being in the course of a single evening, but as one of the actor/spectators announces as he is led off for interrogation, "Tonight we improvised. Tomorrow it is up to you to finish the improvisation" (126).

The relevance and power of *Soirée for the 5th of June* has only grown with time. Viewed from the midst of the Arab Spring, the play is a prescient call to claim the rights of expression and political determination and an attack on the corruption that grew only more extreme and visible as regimes transitioned from socialism to crony capitalism. In Syria, hundreds of thousands have taken up Wannous's invitation to "finish the improvisation," gathering in nightly demonstrations. As in the play, the government has attributed the uprising to the influence of the US and Israel, responding with force as soon as the people claimed their right to define an image of the nation in defiance of the national authority. On September 12, 2011, the United Nations Human Rights Council raised its estimate of the number of protestors killed protesting the government of Bashar Al Assad to 2,600.[11] Protestors' perseverance despite the near certainty of casualties is testimony to the passion they bring to what Wannous termed "our war."

Notes

1. Saadallah Wannous, *Haflat Samar min Ajl 5 Huzayran* [Soirée for the 5th of June], in *al-Aamal al-Kamilah* [The Complete Works] (Damascus: Al Ahali, 1996), vol. 1. Subsequent references to the pages of this publication appear in parentheses in the text. Translations by the author.
2. Saadallah Wannous, *Munamnamat Tarikhiyah* [Historical Miniatures], in *al-Aamal al-Kamilah*, 2:436.
3. That second step is more easily said then done. Wannous's next play, *The Adventures of Jabr the Mamluk's Head* (1970), is literally set in a coffee shop as a storyteller invites his audience to hear more significant stories than mere tales

of Arab heroism. The authorities censored the play after its first performance. Such experiences tempered what Wannous described, in an interview with Marie Elias, as his dream of "discussion inside theatres" and examination of "the fundamental structures of [national] crisis and underdevelopment" as well as his hope that this discussion ultimately would "spread opportunities for democracy and establish the foundations of a civil society." Saadallah Wannous, interview with Marie Elias. "For the First Time I Feel Free to Write; For the First Time I Feel Writing is Enjoyable," *Al Tareeq*, January–February 1992, 101.

4. Patrick Seale, *Asad: The Struggle for the Middle East* (Berkeley: University of California Press, 1989), 143.
5. In the 1927 article "Fetishism," Freud argued that, for the male child, the discovery that women lack a penis produces a deep fear of castration and that fetish objects placate such fear by acting as substitute penises. See Sigmund Freud, *Collected Papers*, vol. 5, *Miscellaneous Papers, 1888–1938* (London: Hogarth and Institute of Psycho-Analysis, 1950), 198–204.
6. Syrian radio announced the fall of Quneitra before fighting even began, prompting an exodus of surrounding villages and confusion among military ranks that, in their disorganization, were getting much of their information from the radio. Seale, *Asad*, 140–41.
7. Karen Shimakawa, *National Abjection: The Asian American Body on Stage* (Durham: Duke University Press, 2002); Maurice E. Stevens, *Troubling Beginnings: Trans(per)forming African-American History and Identity*, Studies in African American History and Culture (New York and London: Routledge, 2003).
8. Julia Kristeva, *Powers of Horror: An Essay on Abjection*, trans. Leon S. Roudiez (New York: Columbia University Press, 1982), 10.
9. Kai T. Erikson, *Everything in Its Path: Destruction of Community in the Buffalo Creek Flood* (New York: Simon and Schuster, 1976), 154.
10. Walter Benjamin, *Illuminations: Essays and Reflections*, ed. Hannah Arendt, trans. Harry Zohn (New York: Schocken Books, 1969), 264.
11. Rick Gladstone, "UN Count of Syrian Dead now at 2,600," *New York Times*, September 12, 2011, www.nytimes.com/2011/09/13/world/middleeast/13syria.html.

3

Saadallah Wannous in Palestine: On and Offstage Performances and Pedagogies

Rania Jawad

At the end of *The Elephant, the King of All Time* by Saadallah Wannous, the actors abandon their character roles and address the audience directly.[1] The point in enacting the story, they tell us succinctly, is for us to collectively learn from the performance. They leave us with questions and also foreshadow a bloodier story to come. Reading the play in the spring of 2011 for a course I teach on modern drama at Birzeit University in the West Bank, students debated the ending – not the content, but its function. Is such an ending necessary? one student questioned. Does such a direct conclusion weaken the story's impact on the audience? another student asked. Can we, the audience, change the course of history? The play's ending provoked a debate about the role of theatre in the world today, defined by the proliferation of new technologies and, more specifically for the students at that historical moment, the popular revolutions across the Arab world.

The play that I was teaching was thus also meant to teach us. While the notion of "teaching plays" is not a new phenomenon, the ways in which theatre and pedagogy intersect in Palestine are revealing.[2] For instance, theatre has been employed as a pedagogical tool by European missionary schools based in Palestine from the mid nineteenth century into the twentieth. Later, it became a tool for the Palestine Liberation Organization (PLO) and other political organizations in the 1960s and 1970s to teach about the national struggle. The proliferation of foreign-funded theatre and drama workshops in the Occupied Palestinian Territories, specifically since the Oslo period in the 1990s, offers insight into the "NGO-ization" of cultural production and how artistic and performance practices are read in globalized circuits. In this essay, I draw on Wannous's writing on the theatre, wherein the role of the audience (whether as spectators, learners, or actors) is privileged, to discuss my experience of teaching *The Elephant, the King of All Time* to Palestinian students as the popular revolutions across the Arab world were unfolding. The story that emerges is one of revolution, reflection, and questioning.

"The Elephant is Dying"[3]

The Elephant, the King of All Time, written in 1969, is a short play based on a four-part structure. In the first part, "The Decision," the people, under the direction of Zakaria, decide to complain to the King about their miserable living conditions, their poverty, and the injustice of their situation. Their major grievance is the King's elephant, running rampant among the people, killing their children haphazardly, and destroying their homes and livelihood. In the second part, "Training," the people practice voicing their complaints before the King; they practice speaking in one voice, rehearsing what it means to be unified. In the third part, "Before the King's Palace," the people await entry to the King's palace, and a King's Guard condescendingly orders them to clean and discipline themselves, restoring them to their role as submissive, inferior subjects of the King. In the fourth and final part, "Before the King," the people are awestruck and immobilized by the grandeur and power of the King, manifested in the numerous palace halls and guards – they are reduced to "silent, bowed bodies."[4] Facing the King alone, Zakaria deforms the people's complaint into a request: the people ask for the elephant to be married in order to relieve his loneliness and to populate the city with his children, tens, hundreds, and thousands of elephants.[5]

While I was teaching the play at Birzeit, classes were disrupted as students gathered in the center of Ramallah to celebrate the Egyptian people's success in overthrowing their expired president and to support the Libyan people in the face of brutal regime violence.[6] Back in class, students analyzed the role of the young girl in Wannous's play. Unnamed and representative of the next generation, her part consists simply of asking a few questions. The girl's straightforward yet revealing questions, however, serve to interrogate the status quo and thus the injustice of the present. "But why does the King love a vicious elephant?" she asks her mother, after hearing of the death, destruction, and misery inflicted on the people by the King's elephant. "Where's the King hiding away?" she asks as they enter the King's palace, passing through the halls, door after door, each manned by a group of stone-faced guards. While the character of Zakaria takes the lead in mobilizing the people to action, the students identified the role of the young girl as key to understanding the cyclical nature of the play's story.

In the play, the people's dismissal of the young girl's questions and her frightened mother's eventual silencing of her voice – for example, she puts her hand over the girl's mouth to prevent her from speaking in front of the King – sustain the status quo. Familiar to other times and places, the authority's oppressive regime immobilizes the community, trickling down to the very hands and mouths of the people. Although she is meant to inherit the fear and silence of the older generation, the young girl came to represent for my students the millions of protestors taking over public squares across the Arab world to demand voice in governance, justice, dignity, and in Palestine a third intifada. The actors who address the audience at the end of the enacted story carry the role of the girl offstage, provoking the audience with questions and the responsibility to intervene in the cycle of violence and oppression.

At the end of the semester, the young girl appeared again in class, this time in an adaptation of Wannous's play, written collectively and performed by four of my students. Before their performance, Maisa, the actress playing Zakaria, addressed the audience of students, directing them when to exclaim and when to shush, according to the various signs she would hold up. We rehearsed following her lead until she was satisfied with our performance. At the climax of the students' play, we, the audience, obeyed Zakaria's signs as the King (played by Nida) strutted before his subjects in finely woven dress, imaginatively sewn out of air by two characters resembling *Waiting for Godot*'s Vladimir and Estragon (played by Manar and Samya). However, another student in class, Ala, began to laugh loudly and mockingly. Despite our confusion as to whether Ala was an actor in the play in the role of an audience member, her intervention denuded the King of his cloak as well as of his power over the audience. While the learned silence of the people is imposed on Wannous's young girl, in our class Ala's laugh was contagious.

Relocating the moment of directly addressing the audience in Wannous's play from the end to the beginning, following Maisa's directions, the students not only brought the audience members into the performances but also cast and directed our role. We praised the King when told to exclaim and were silent when told to be quiet. We learned that it took very little to create an obedient audience. As another student Naseem pointed out, because the people played the role of an audience before the King in Wannous's play, thus obeying the rules of authority set for them, they failed Zakaria and were not able to break the cycle of top-down violence that maintained the status quo. We also learned that the laughter of a sole young girl can be powerful enough to publicly humiliate a figure of authority, thus undermining the power dynamics at play in the moment. It was also Ala's contagious laughter that broke our obedience and allowed us to freely express ourselves. "It is a vigorous blow to vices," Molière writes in the preface to his play *Tartuffe*, "to expose them to public laughter." Resonating with Molière's sentiments that we had read in class together the semester before, the students put into practice such a strategy: "Criticism is taken lightly, but men will not tolerate satire. They are quite willing to be mean, but they never like to be ridiculed."[7]

Humor and satire are elements that a number of commentators noted during the Egyptian people's revolution that successfully overthrew Hosni Mubarak. Photographs of the numerous signs protestors made and held circulated globally, as did political caricatures and jokes. In another play written by a student in my class, she draws on jokes that were circulating in online forums regarding Mubarak's public address in response to the people's popular revolts. She adapted a turning point in Wannous's play, the interaction with the King's Guard before the people enter the King's palace, to the contemporary context of revolution we were witnessing and living. Dima's one-act play, titled *The Crowds are Waiting*, comprised a short dialogue between a President and his Guard, exploring how a simple and brief interaction can be the catalyst for a dramatic turn of events.

> Guard (*in a rushed voice*): Sir, the crowds are waiting.
> President: Waiting?
> Guard: For your speech.
> President: Oh, indeed they are.
> Guard: Excuse my curiosity sir, but what are you planning to tell them?
> President: Haven't made up my mind yet.
> Guard: Planning to improvise?
> President: It's not like there's much to improvise anyway. The people have decided.
> Guard: Since when do they get to decide?
> President: Been asking myself the same question lately.
> Guard: And?
> President: I haven't come up with an answer yet.
> Guard: Planning to renounce the throne?
> President: That or ... the people.
> Guard: I beg your pardon?

Dima's three-page play ties the authoritative positioning of leaders in power for decades to a patriarchal "civilizing" discourse that undermines any belief in people's ability to self-govern. As it is not until the very end of the play that the impact of the President's dialogue with his Guard is revealed (which I will not disclose here), the structure mirrors Wannous's play in which the people's interaction with the King's Guard outside the palace gates sets the stage for the unexpected ending.

In both student plays, the endings transformed the failure that we encounter at the end of Wannous's story. Or we can say that the students translated the direct address of Wannous's actors at the end of his play into their own. In the words of Naseem regarding the potential of theatre, the students learned from Wannous "how to rebuild, recreate, and how to write their endings by their own hands." The students thus accompany the millions of people in the streets revolting against leaders that do not represent their interests but rather systematically and violently oppress them; they are calling for the death of the King's elephant. In a recent commentary marking the 14th anniversary of Wannous's death – Wannous passed away on May 15, the day Palestinians mark as the Nakba – the author describes the contemporary Arab revolutions as "the beginning of the end of the era of the elephant in the Arab world."[8] Just as students make theatre in response to current political changes, so too are political events analyzed through theatre. Decades after Wannous wrote *The Elephant, the King of All Time*, actors in the streets were able to accomplish what those in the play could not.

The Elephant in the Textbook

Perhaps because of its continued importance and the critique it levels of a phenomenon prevalent in the Arab world through the decades, *The Elephant, the King of All Time* was included in what has been referred to as the "first"

Palestinian national curriculum, created under the Palestinian Authority as a product of the Oslo Accords.[9] Initiated in the late 1990s, the curriculum was progressively introduced into schools in the West Bank and Gaza Strip from 2000 to 2006. The final lesson in the Arabic language and literature textbook used in the last year of high school (*tawjihi*) is on the genre of theatre and includes Wannous's play. The version of the play printed in the Palestinian textbook, however, gives the last word to the King. "Your request will be granted," he says in response to Zakaria's request to find the King's elephant a wife and populate the city with their offspring. "You may go," he responds to the people, laughing.[10] The textbook version thus ends with the enacted story before the actors comment on the pedagogy of the play.

Omitting the actors' direct address following the King's dismissal of his subjects leaves the power in the hands of the King while also removing a reflexive device of theatre. Both, in effect, serve to disempower the audience, whether by indirect association with the people who are immobilized or by removing direct reference to the audience's intervention in the story. The pedagogy of the play rests on a belief in the audience to reflect on the questions put forth and to intervene in the course of events, which the actors – and Wannous – predict to be even bloodier. By omitting the direct address ending, the textbook, on the other hand, leans more toward a passive role for the audience, based on a pedagogy of right and wrong answers and memorization, as evidenced by the textbook analysis following the play and the subsequent questions for students to answer. Although the altered ending in the textbook is most likely a case of "simplifying" the teaching and study of theatre, the omission is significant.

What the textbook offers is one example of how theatre is taught to Palestinian students, in this case graduating high school students in the West Bank and Gaza Strip. As is generally the case in "national" and streamlined curriculums, the knowledge and experience of the students is not part of the learning process. The most basic and essential component in the educational process is therefore left out. The discussion on the genre of theatre, however, is more complex. Addressing the "absence of theatre in Arab culture historically," the textbook lists some of the main reasons put forth by Arab and Western Orientalist scholars alike: the geographical environment and nomadic culture, the nature of the Arab mind, and the religious factor.[11] Each of these arguments is followed by a question meant to challenge the assumptions behind it and then concludes by advocating a more comprehensive understanding that includes internal and external "social, economic, political, literary, artistic, and local factors."

Although adhering to an East/West dichotomy and the discourse of genesis ("Researchers agree that the birth of modern Arab theatre was 1847 in Syria ..."), the narrative in the textbook exposes its readers to a dominant approach to Arab societies and cultures. It also performs the act of questioning ideas and perspectives put forth, specifically by academic scholarship. The few pages devoted to theatre at the end of the book could then have guided the reader to an understanding that such Orientalist perspectives, whether expressed via scholarship or literature, serve larger interests that result in dire political actions and aggression impacting us, the readers of the text. Such a return to the audience, as we see in the actors' address at the end of *The Elephant, the King of All Time*, makes a clear and direct link between theatre and audience, pedagogy and our lives.

Offstage Pedagogy

The technique of commentary on the performance contained within the play itself is one that Wannous develops in a number of his plays, specifically because it enables a critical reflection not only on the content of the story being enacted but also on the theatre as well. In Wannous's writings on the theatre, from his "Manifestos for a New Arab Theatre," published in 1970, to the address he delivered on World Theatre Day in 1996, a year before his death, he privileges the experience of the audience.[12] Although the direct politicization (*tasees*) of his earlier writings takes a form closer to critical reflection at the end of his life, perhaps due more to the devastations in the Arab world than to Wannous's own deteriorating health, the focus on the audience's role in the theatre is based on its resonance beyond the realm of the theatre. What is gained *in* the theatre is meant to be carried *out* of the theatre space.

No matter what technological revolutions the theatre undergoes, Wannous said in his 1996 address, the theatre will continue to offer a forum in which we can contemplate our "historical and existential" condition together in a communal context. The multiplicity of dialogues that take place before, during, and after the theatre performance, he articulates, is what activates and makes manifest community affiliation, collectivity, and civil society. Wannous's speech in 1996 is essentially an assessment of the place of theatre in our increasingly technologically mediated and "globalized" world. The assessment is grim, for culture as Wannous envisions it has been marginalized in favor of increasing inequalities, aggression, and social divisions.

As we see in Palestine and elsewhere, the flow of ideas, people, and technologies across borders of nation and language, while often lauded as the progress of globalization, also implies the global circulation of racist ideologies, settler colonialism, and borders that are disappearing only for communities of privilege. New concrete borders and walls are being built while old ones are often renamed or reconfigured rather than torn down. In Palestine, the "globalized" version of the world we are living in reflects both Israel's use of global tools such as military armament, United Nations vetoes, and the further isolation and ghettoization of the Palestinian population. Teaching the text of Wannous's 1996 speech in class in conjunction with his play and other plays written in the twentieth century – years defined by brutal, destructive wars, ongoing colonialism, ethnic cleansing, and the technological advances that alter our relationship to time and space – has been as much about situating ourselves in the world today as it has been about analyzing the role of theatre.

The question of theatre in Palestine has been approached in numerous and diverse ways by theatre practitioners, cultural commentators, and community-based and development organizations, among others. Theatre in the service of national liberation – as a tool for addressing Palestinian social issues, as a measurement of neoliberal ideology, or as a threat to the "security" of the Israeli state – provides examples of certain frames used to read theatre in Palestine. Here, I discuss the practice of theatre in a refugee camp in the northern West Bank to offer another perspective on the intersection of cultural production, pedagogy, and revolutionary change. Evoking Wannous's vision, I focus my discussion on how the practice of theatre in Jenin refugee camp extends beyond its walls, beyond the individual, and beyond the local community.

Echoing Wannous's words in his 1996 speech, actor and director Juliano Mer Khamis described the practice of theatre in Palestine as one of rebuilding: "Theatre makes community," he said. "You need timetables, division of labor, responsibility, solidarity – it's a model society. Along the way, the process rebuilds the communication tools that have broken down as the society has been broken."[13] And he meant this literally as well as metaphorically. Mer Khamis described a new generation of Palestinian youth who "have lost their language," the inability to speak and express themselves. He specifically spoke of the children and youth of Jenin refugee camp who have been severely impacted by decades-long violent Israeli policies of collective punishment and local social fragmentation. For these reasons, Mer Khamis came to the camp in the early 1990s with his mother Arna to establish a space for theatre and other creative and educational projects.

This experience was captured in the documentary film he produced in 2003, *Arna's Children*. Following the death of his mother to cancer and the

Israeli army's destruction of the theatre she created, Mer Khamis returned to the camp and established the Freedom Theatre in 2006. According to him, the main aim of the theatre, built upon Arna's work, is to provide the children and youth of the camp with a space to "develop the skills, self-knowledge, and confidence which can empower them to challenge present realities" and to reach out beyond the limits of their own community.[14] Making theatre thus becomes a form of empowerment and pedagogical practice, a process that encourages the youth of the camp to imagine beyond what they know, to "rearrange" reality, in the words of theatre.

Within the post-Oslo context, where the cultural sphere in the West Bank and Gaza Strip has undergone a process of NGO-ization and transformations due to the large influx of foreign-funded projects and "expertise," the goals of the Freedom Theatre remain focused on serving the local community of the camp. As foreign donors attempt to reconfigure the stage of the theatre into a pedagogical tool to address social issues, most often within frameworks of humanitarianism and "nonviolence," the needs of the Palestinian population are reprioritized and decontextualized. Based on a model of non-isolationalism, encouraging Palestinians from both inside Israel and the West Bank to participate as instructors, actors, and spectators while inviting international volunteers and funders to serve the needs of the Theatre, the practice of the Freedom Theatre remains politically contextualized within a framework of resistance, resilience, and self-development.

On the evening of April 7, 2011, a public screening of *Arna's Children* was organized in Manara Square, the most central location in Ramallah. The screening took place directly following the performance of a play that Juliano Mer Khamis had directed and three days after he was murdered.[15] In addition to members of the theatre community, more than 100 passers-by stood for more than an hour to watch the documentary that recounts the story of the young boys active in the cultural center that Arna established during the First Intifada. We see the young boys as they speak about and perform in the theatre, and the film follows Mer Khamis as he returns to Jenin during the Israeli invasion and destruction of the camp in 2002, where nearly all of his former students are now dead.

I have seen the film before, but this particular viewing in Manara was especially striking.[16] For as I watched the film projected on the screen, I also watched Mer Khamis's current theatre students among the audience. The juxtaposition of the story of theatre in Jenin refugee camp from the First Intifada to today, five years after the theatre space was rebuilt and a professional acting school was inaugurated in 2008, complicates a linear understanding not only of the role of theatre but also of resistance to military occupation and colonial rule.[17] Binaries of art versus violence and actor versus audience break down, and the relationship between on and offstage can no longer be read as distinct. The multiplicity of dialogues Wannous spoke of was alive as people in the street unconnected to theatre in Palestine discussed and debated the film.

While the King's elephant in *The Elephant, the King of All Time* is a direct translation of the violence against the people in the play, the different forms of oppression at play in the context of Jenin refugee camp and Palestine in general cannot be consolidated into one figurative symbol, no matter how large. Just as the silencing of a young girl is not only caused by a hand cupped over her mouth, the people cannot be read as one group, unified either in protest or in fear. "We are all responsible for the destruction of Palestine," Mer Khamis said, and "we must take responsibility."[18] The question of how we are responsible cannot be understood by any one reading; however, in calling ourselves responsible, we all have the potential to act. Screening *Arna's Children* in Manara that evening brought to the fore with a brute simplicity questions of the Palestinian struggle, resistance to different forms of Israeli aggression toward Palestinian society, and the place of art and theatre in a context characterized by extreme violence. The context is also one marked by a resilience to rebuild and what can perhaps be called a delayed hope.

* * *

Teaching Wannous is also about how Wannous teaches us. Wannous in Palestine evokes a pedagogy that encourages us to reflect on the roles we play in the performances of power acted out in Israel and Palestine. The study and practice of theatre, whether in the classroom, the theatre, or beyond those walls, should generate questions that encourage awareness and analysis, self-reflection, and change. And the notion of hope means imagining alternatives to the status quo and their potential realization. It is about "rearranging reality."

Notes

1. Saadallah Wannous, *al-Fil ya Malik al-Zaman wa Mughamarat Ras al-Mamluk Jabr* [The Elephant, the King of All Time and The Adventures of Jabr the Mamluk's Head] (Beirut: Dar Al Adab, 1977). An English translation titled *The King's Elephant* can be found in Salma Khadra Jayyusi, ed., *Short Arabic Plays: An Anthology* (New York: Interlink Books, 2003), 433–51.
2. Although my discussion here largely focuses on theatre in the Occupied Palestinian Territories, the relationship between theatre and pedagogy for Palestinian artists inside the Green Line is also fertile ground for analysis.
3. This refers to the title of a recent commentary written to commemorate the anniversary of Wannous's death. See Brahim El Guabli, "In Memory of Saadallah Wannous ... The Elephant is Dying," *Jadaliyya*, May 18, 2011, in Arabic.
4. Wannous, *The King's Elephant*, 449.
5. In class, the students offered a particularly local interpretation of Zakaria's request. Marrying off a young bachelor carries connotations of settling him down, of taming. While the interpretation is not restricted to the Palestinian context, on-the-ground politics in Palestine make distinctive use of this notion. Policies of the Israeli military occupation distinguish between married and unmarried men, for instance with regards to issuing permits for entry and work within Israel and its West Bank settlements.
6. Birzeit University is approximately 15–20 minutes' drive from the center of Ramallah.

7. W. B. Worthen, ed., *The Harcourt Brace Anthology of Drama*, 2nd edn. (New York: Harcourt Brace College Publishers, 1996), 432.
8. El Guabli, "In Memory of Saadallah Wannous."
9. Following the establishment of Israel in 1948, schools in the West Bank followed a Jordanian education curriculum, and schools in the Gaza Strip adhered to an Egyptian curriculum. After the military occupation of the Palestinian territories in 1967, Israel controlled Palestinian education, maintaining the two separate curricula and censoring material that was disapproved. For information on the Palestinian national curriculum currently in place, see Palestinian Curriculum Development Center, "Home," accessed May 29, 2011, www.pcdc.edu.ps. I was not aware that Wannous's play was part of the curriculum when I chose to teach the play at Birzeit.
10. *The Arabic Language: Reading, Literature, and Criticism* (Ramallah: Palestinian Ministry of Education and Higher Learning, 2006).
11. For one clear example, see Mohammed A. Al Khozai, *The Development of Early Arabic Drama 1847–1900* (New York: Longman, 1984).
12. Saadallah Wannous, *Bayanat li Masrah Arabi Jadeed* [Manifestos for a New Arab Theatre] (Beirut: Dar Al Fikr Al Jadeed, 1988); Saadallah Wannous, "In Memoriam: Theater and the Thirst for Dialogue," *Middle East Report*, 203 (1997), 14–15.
13. Alisa Solomon, "Rehearsing for Freedom," *American Theatre* (May/June 2008), 82.
14. See the Freedom Theatre, "Home," May 29, 2011, www.thefreedomtheatre.org.
15. Juliano Mer Khamis was murdered on April 4, 2011, in his car outside the Freedom Theatre in Jenin refugee camp. It is still unclear who is responsible.
16. In my first encounter with the film, I learned that I had met the mother of one of the main characters in the film and had in my possession his picture as he holds his newborn baby, taken days before he was killed by the Israeli army. At the time, I was visiting Jenin refugee camp in the summer of 2003 before *Arna's Children* had been released.
17. The Freedom Theatre's Acting School is a three-year full-time program, inaugurated in September 2008 in partnership with the Arab American University in Jenin. For more information, see the Freedom Theatre, "Acting School," May 29, 2011, www.thefreedomtheatre.org/active-school.php.
18. These words are taken from a video recording made in support of the Freedom Theatre, which was screened at a memorial for Juliano Mer Khamis in Al Midan Theatre, Haifa, May 21, 2011.

4

Performance through the Egyptian Revolution: Stories from Tahrir

Dalia Basiouny

The newfound sense of possibility inspired by the revolutions of the Arab Spring was reflected in the surge of artistic and cultural expression that began in January 2011. It flourished during the 18 days of demonstrations in Tahrir Square and throughout Egypt and continued through the following months. Change and self-governance, once distant dreams, became feasible and within reach. Theatre and performance honored the revolution and its heroes, capturing the spirit of a chant from the revolution, "Raise your head high, you are Egyptian!"

One of the first performances to register the events of the revolution was the documentary theatre piece *Tahrir Stories*, a compilation of testimonies by revolutionaries about their experiences, which opened in late February 2011. I collected these stories, molded them into a performance text, and performed the piece with Sabeel for the Arts,[1] the independent theatre group I established in 1997.

The early days of the revolution were full of hope, both on and off the stage. In her review of *Tahrir Stories* and similar post-revolutionary theatre productions[2] in the spring of 2011, theatre critic and scholar Nehad Selaiha wrote:

> In all, one major theme was "breaking the barrier of fear and feeling empowered." Another was recovering a sense of belonging to something called Egypt and taking pride in the fact, together with a sense of dignity and personal worth. If the revolution has done nothing else and achieves nothing in future, this would be enough and well worth all the sacrifices.[3]

In this essay, I write about my experiences as a theatre maker during the Egyptian Revolution of 2011 and trace the process of creating and performing *Tahrir Stories*. I begin by exploring the creative process and then present the unique circumstances of the first four performances of this piece. I also look at the dynamics of performing live theatre during an intense political moment and explore how the revolution disrupts plays about the revolution.

Process: Collecting the Stories

Before the revolution launched on January 25, 2011, I was rehearsing a play[4] that I wrote two years before, but after the Friday of Wrath,[5] something major shifted in Egypt. I began participating in the demonstrations in Tahrir Square and started to hear stories, accounts of what happened or what was happening. The stories varied in urgency and gravity – from diverting thugs and providing food and medicine to bearing witness to the death of a friend or the survival of a demonstrator.

In my roles both as citizen and as theatre artist, I felt the need to collect the myriad stories for those who participated in the revolution to know more about what took place, for non-demonstrators to get a feeling of what was going on, and for the future. I started collecting first-person accounts through taped interviews and distributed a set of 20 questions through email and Facebook. I would later use these stories in what came to be my first documentary performance, *Tahrir Stories*.

The piece attempted to register the history of the revolution as it was unfolding, so we had to prepare and present the performance as quickly and efficiently as possible. As we worked, the counter-revolution emerged as an attempt to stymie the force of the popular uprising, and the clash of these opposing socio-political forces resulted in incidents that disrupted performances of the play. The play continued to evolve in response to current events – we adapted to diverse locations, production circumstances, and ongoing revolution dynamics, all of which were reflected in modifications to the script and our performances.

The Premiere: Hanager Arts Center

The first performance of *Tahrir Stories* took place on February 23, 2011, at Hanager Arts Center. The president had been ousted on February 11, but as the regime was still in power, demonstrations continued to ensure that the demands of the revolution were met. Cairo traffic was exceptionally difficult on our opening night. People who were supposed to help in setting up the performance arrived after the end of the show, and many audience members were stuck for hours and returned to their homes. We later learned that a fire had erupted in the upper floors of the Ministry of the Interior, causing traffic mayhem.

Located on the grounds of the Opera House, Hanager Arts Center is half a mile from Tahrir Square; it has been closed for renovations for the past two years. Dr. Hoda Wasfy, the manager of this theatre complex, suggested that independent artists who were interested in presenting work inspired by the spirit of the Tahrir could use the open area in front of the building under construction. And so we did. I organized a series of five events under the title "Evenings from the Square," which included music and theatre performances.

They were well attended, and the audience did not mind standing to watch performances or seeing the site's background of sand and gravel, which unintentionally evoked the familiar atmosphere of Tahrir Square.

Sabeel for the Arts presented *Tahrir Stories* for the first time in the context of this series. We had very little time for rehearsals, as most of us were going to marches, creating coalitions, and running from one political meeting to the next in an attempt to activate the revolution in our respective fields.

Our main challenge during the rehearsal process was organizing the material we had collected. We decided on a chronological sequence, though most testimonies moved back and forth through time, narrating more than one event. Testimonies about the marches of January 25 and 28 came first. These were followed by accounts of the horrors that demonstrators faced in order to take over Tahrir Square and to defend the Egyptian Museum. The next scene comprised a testimony about the armed attacks against demonstrators on February 2, in what came to be known as the Battle of the Camels.[6] The final scene narrated stories of the lost and of martyrs, concluding with bittersweet celebrations of the ex-president's ousting. Some of the accounts overlapped, but each presented a unique element in the mosaic of narratives of the Egyptian Revolution.

The set was simple: two cotton rugs and some straw chairs from home. Hanager provided three microphones to help project the sound into the open-air space. I set up the evening as a ritual, with candles, incense, voices, and sound. We delineated the performance space with the rugs and surrounded both the "stage" and the "standing auditorium" with tea-light candles in transparent plastic cups. We started burning the incense and waited for the construction workers renovating the Opera House to stop so that we could begin the introductory sound ritual. They ignored our motions and continued mixing cement and moving wood. So, we began the ritual performance – honoring those who died by reciting their names and performing the stories of those who survived the 18-day revolution – against the backdrop of construction clamor.

Using a Tibetan singing ball and an Egyptian flute, we attempted to create a soundscape to transform the space and take the audience on a journey that followed the steps of the rebels in Tahrir Square and other locations. There were eight performers, two musicians, and a few people helping with the setup, all dressed in black while the veiled women wore white headscarves. I adorned everyone's costume with a ribbon of the Egyptian flag's colors, a popular symbol from Tahrir.

The first performance featured eight testimonies. Four of us read our own testimonies, and the rest of the actors read testimonies penned by others who had attended the first performance. At the end of the piece, each performer recited names of martyrs. There were 196 names identified at that time (the number later reached 900). Each name was followed by a drumbeat. At the end of the naming ritual, the performers hummed together, and their voices joined in a loud scream that reverberated in the air, resonating as they exited the "stage" to walk toward the audience and merge with them, refusing to create space for an ovation.

The power of that performance was in its raw quality and its immediacy. Some of the first-person accounts moved the audience to tears. The stories culminated in the final testimony by Manar Ahmad. Ahmad described her encounter with the mother of a young man who died during the revolution. The bereaved mother was celebrating the honorable death of her son to free his country until she heard the third speech by Mubarak, who refused to step down. Her celebration turned to mourning as she felt that her son lost his life in vain. When the news of Mubarak's resignation reached Tahrir Square on February 11, 2011, her jubilant ululation trembled across the square – and was echoed on stage by other performers.

The Second Performance: Helwan University

In March, the Faculty of Arts at Helwan University was preparing an event to welcome students back after the extended mid-term recess, longer than the recess of other universities because of the delays resulting from lack of security at Helwan. One of the theatre professors, who attended the performance of *Tahrir Stories*, suggested inviting the documentary play to be featured in the celebrations, scheduled for March 15, 2011.

In preparation for this performance, we added two new testimonies, and I decided not to perform my own. The elevated stage was set in the middle of the main walkway of the university, and a DJ was playing nationalist and revolutionary songs nearby. Since it was midday, we could not use candles or incense, so I decided to rely on human voices to create the ritual aspect of the performance. I recruited a number of my students in the theatre department and trained them on the day of the performance. Their humming and voice toning created a musical background for the piece as well as a link between the testimonies.

Our group looked powerful, with eight performers and twelve chorus members in black, walking single file with focused intent to the stage area. The performers lined the stage while the chorus members stood in two rows on both sides of the stage. This open-air festivity drew many passers-by. As the performance progressed in the midday heat without music or drumbeats, only a few dedicated audience members were keenly following the accounts. The organizers of the event were unhappy with the thinning audience and asked us to "take a break" for the DJ to play loud music and attract more attendees. After multiple requests from the organizers, I decided to cut the performance short and signaled to the actors onstage to end their performance halfway through.

After we left the stage, we realized that much the audience had left earlier to join the protest against the President of the Helwan, scheduled at the same time as the performance. Some of the performers suggested that the timing of our performance and the whole celebration was planned to distract students from marching and protesting. We joined the protestors at the offices of the President, channeling our energy and our voices toward a more overt political cause – removing the President who was appointed by the previous regime and refused to leave his office, in spite of regular demonstrations demanding his resignation.

The Third Performance: Manf Theatre

Our theatre group, along with three other independent groups, was invited to participate in an event celebrating the revolution and organized by the government-run Manf Theatre, one of the Ministry of Culture's Cultural Palaces. Manf is an open-air space with the stage set on one side of a courtyard. It is surrounded by other theatre buildings, including the Balloon Theatre and National Circus. Employees of the theatre often spend time in the open auditorium, chatting or debating politics – and they continued their arguments even during our performance!

Our simple technical requirements were met by a number of worried phone calls and email messages, primarily because of our request to use candles.[7] As no candles or incense would be allowed in the theatre, we relied once again on the human voice to support the introductory ritual. I invited dozens of people to join the chorus. It was the evening of March 20, 2011, and a sense of unease and anxiety hung thick in the air. The results of the referendum on constitutional amendments had been announced the night before, upsetting many of the performers who were active during the revolution and hoped for a majority vote against passing the amendments.[8] To many activists, even more frustrating than the results themselves were the tactics and political schemes used to manipulate the population, taking advantage of the illiteracy of the majority of the Egyptians.

I used rehearsal as an opportunity to work through that anger with voice exercises. The cast members, the chorus, and some of their friends channeled the political news into creative energy to carry us through the performance. It was an exciting process, as most of them had never sung or even raised their voices before. They were learning to liberate their breath, their voices, and their bodies for the first time. Some of them cried while many laughed with relief as their voices soared above the open-air theatre. We played a number of voice and energy games, and our voices reverberated through the space before and after the performance.

We set chairs on stage for the performers and placed the standing chorus in the auditorium behind the audience in an attempt to surround the space and close it vocally. We used two microphones, hoping that they would carry the voices of the performers into the open-air space and be louder than the atmosphere created by the theatre employees and surrounding theatres. We encountered a few difficulties during the performance. One of the actors abused the microphone with a loud and overly dramatic presentation, and there was distance between the stage and the seats, creating a sense of separation between the performers and audience and swallowing the voice of the chorus in the air. Despite these obstacles, the ritual energy, which began before the audience entered and drew to a close after they left, saved the performance. In this third rendition of *Tahrir Stories*, what happened on the stage became just one element of a larger ritual that the performers enacted in the space, regardless of the audience.

The Fourth Performance: Manf Theatre

The next day brought new turbulence to Cairo, and traffic was disastrous. It was Mother's Day, March 21, 2011, but the culprit was another fire in the Ministry of the Interior, which paralyzed the city. Most of the chorus members were not able come to the theatre. The actors were very late, and a few arrived as we were ready to go on stage. Without a chorus and with an incomplete cast, I felt it would be better to cancel the performance and left the decision to the group.

A number of the actors wished to perform, while others felt that the situation precluded a meaningful interpretation of the piece. This was not simply a pastiche of monologues but a ritual that transformed our energy as a group of artists before transforming the energy of the broader audience. Since most of the group wanted to do the performance and a few audience members had braved Cairo traffic to attend, I decided to create a new performance to suit the changing circumstances.

I moved the audience onstage to separate them from the hubbub of the Manf Theatre employees and did away with the microphones. I created a semicircle with the seats of the audience to engulf the performers, who sat on the floor to close the audience's circle. With no musical instruments, no chorus (only two chorus members made it to the theatre that night), and no microphones, I used a copper singing bowl to evoke the sense of ritual and to act as a connection between the testimonies. Since the actor who would have started the performance was still stuck in traffic, we needed a new beginning. Luckily I had the text of my other play, *Solitaire*, a one-woman performance that also dealt with the revolution, and decided to use it.

The physical closeness to the audience created a solid sense of connection: the audience surrounded the performers, and the actor sharing a testimony stood in the center of the audience. This encouraged audience members to engage more closely with the performers, commenting and asking questions. Stripping theatre to its bare bones worked in this performance without pretense or production technicalities – just the actor, audience, and story. The proximity of actor and audience created intimacy, and the strength of the stories moved the audience. The testimonies recreated the sense of urgency that prevailed in Tahrir.

Mustafa Mahmoud, reading the testimony of Hassan Abu Bakr, gave a particularly gripping performance. The story captured the sense of jubilation and uncertainty that coursed through Egypt the night of Mubarak's resignation six weeks prior:

> I didn't spend nights at the square because I had to check up on my daughter who was very pregnant and past her due date. On February 11, I was standing in front of the operating room. They called me to watch the speech of the vice president on TV. The president stepped down, and my daughter gave birth! I saw baby Laila and then left the hospital to the street. I saw a porter and his son – I said, "Congratulations." They were really scared. They have never known a president other than Mubarak! I told them, "Don't worry. Tomorrow, we will have a better president. And it doesn't matter who comes next, what matters more is how he is chosen."
>
> ...
>
> I walked in the streets alone, shouting: "Viva Egypt, viva Egypt! Egypt is now free, Egypt is free!" I walked toward the Nile, shouting: "The Egyptian people toppled the regime!" Suddenly, I found young people shouting behind me. A crowd gathered and chanted as we walked. Everyone was going to the sacred heart, Tahrir Square, all of us shouting "Viva Egypt!"[9]

This simple performance was a message of hope for the audience, reminding them that change is possible, and that the people who succeeded in creating the revolution would continue to demand and enact change.

Four Stories

The four performances of *Tahrir Stories* presented in February and March 2011 differed in energy, tone, and aesthetics just as the relationship between actors and audiences varied depending on our location. Regardless of the changes in set-up, aesthetics, and even in the testimonies, the piece affected the audience. Though it premiered less than two weeks after the ousting of the president, it worked as a reminder of the events of the revolution: the detailed accounts and testimonies mixed the personal and the political, illustrating how the performers and demonstrators themselves changed over the 18 days of the Egyptian Revolution. These first-hand accounts gave a taste of Tahrir Square to audience members who did not demonstrate, while refreshing demonstrators' memories of the events they witnessed and experienced.

A few dedicated activists told me after the first performance how grateful they were for the reminder of why they went out to fight initially and how they must continue until the demands of the people are fully met. One woman sent us her eyewitness account of the snipers around the Square, describing the way in which they aimed at the rebels' heads or hearts. She conveyed the heroism of those who entered the line of fire to retrieve martyrs killed by the snipers. This phenomenon was not unique to our project. For instance, the creators of *Tahrir Monologues*,[10] another performance that uses testimonies from rebels and demonstrators, also had audience members approach them after performances to share their own stories. Sometimes, spectators volunteered to relate their accounts of the revolution in future productions. Audiences wanted to share their own stories and testimonies of the revolution, blurring the line between audience and performer, as both have become enlivened in a society awakening to a new wave of activism.

Notes

1. The group adopted its name from the restored *sabeel* (water fountain) where we performed our first piece. Sabeel's mission is to promote women's work and present new non-traditional work in alternative performance spaces. I revived the group upon my return to Cairo from New York in 2009.

2. One such example is the theatre group Halwasa's *By the Light of the Revolution Moon*, written and acted by Hani Abdel Naser, Mohamed Abdel Muiz, and Ahmed Fuad, and directed by Hani Abdel Naser.
3. Nehad Selaiha, "Tahrir Tales," *Al Ahram Weekly*, 1042, 7–13 April, 2011.
4. In summer 2009, I wrote *Solitaire*, a play about three Egyptian women from the same family. The play has since been revised to include a new section about the Egyptian Revolution, and I have been touring the new version as a one-woman show in Egypt and abroad since March 2011.
5. Friday, January 28, 2011, witnessed major clashes between demonstrators and security forces in many cities in Egypt. Because of the extreme violence of the police and the random killing of peaceful demonstrators, it came to be known as the "Friday of Wrath."
6. While the media referred to the events of February 2, 2011, as the Battle of the Camels, many of the rebels called it *Mowqeat al-Gahsh* (Battle of the Little Donkey), belittling the attackers and adding humor to the situation. The rebels even exhibited war trophies from the battle, hanging a saddle, some shoes, and items of clothing they collected from the attacks on a lamp post with a sign that read, "Museum of the Battle of the Little Donkey."
7. Cairo experienced a major tragedy in 2008 when more than 100 audience members died in a fire in the Egyptian National Theatre in Ataba Square. Since that incident, the theatre authorities refuse to allow any open flame on stage, even though most theatre workers smoke inside the building, onstage, and in the workshops.
8. The Military Council in charge of the transitional government in Egypt decided to hold a referendum on March 19, 2011, for people to vote on six constitutional amendments. These forbade the president from staying in office for more than two terms and prevented him from passing the country's leadership on to his son. Though both are important matters, these amendments did not address many of the issues the rebels wanted to see changed. Nonetheless, it was the highest turnout for a vote in Egyptian history, with more than 18 million people going to the ballot boxes. But there were many tactics used to divide the society between liberals and conservatives, as well as between Muslims and Christians. The results of the referendum were disappointing to many activists who thought that after the successful revolution, things would change in their favor.
9. Hassan Abu Bakr's testimony of February 11, 2011.
10. See Rowan Al Shimi, "Tahrir Monologues: A Trip Back in Time to the 18 Days that Changed Egypt," *Ahram Online*, May 27, 2011, http://english.ahram.org.eg.

5

Three Egyptian Plays in the Wake of the January Revolution

Samia Habib

From the Puppet Theatre in Cairo to the public squares of Suez, the theatres and performance sites of Egypt buzzed with narratives of liberation in the spring of 2011 following the January Revolution. Mainly amateurs, first-time directors, and novice playwrights as well as some theatre veterans took to the stages and produced shows, sometimes hastily thrown together and sometimes conceptually one-dimensional, that denounced the fallen Mubarak regime and lauded the revolution. The performances tended to be documentary in nature. During this period, Egyptian theatre artists engaged in political dialogue about topics such as the constitutional referendum and the widespread corruption and nepotism that characterized the government. Above all, Egyptian theatre acknowledged the martyrs and victims of the revolution, honoring their sacrifices and preserving their stories in collective memory.

Deploying theatre as a mechanism of political commentary and resistance has a long history in the Arab world. Since the mid twentieth century, when the colonial order crumbled and nascent rulers sought to consolidate power over newly formed nation-states, those who critiqued the ruling regimes have suffered oppression and censorship. Only a lucky handful were ever granted political leeway; the regimes in Egypt and elsewhere often pointed to these few artists to indicate a misleading extent of freedom of expression and democracy. Otherwise, the state tended to support theatre which glorified the ruling authority and enhanced its legitimacy.

In the months following Mubarak's ousting, I attended a number of performances in Cairo, Suez, Port Said, and other cities throughout Egypt. Many of these projects were independently organized and self-financed, and some were presented free of charge. Three productions – *Hikayat Meedan* (Story of the Square), *Kharabeesh* (Scratches), and *Al Jeel Abu Zalouma* (The Long Trunk Generation) – indicate the diverse ways in which Egyptian theatre artists registered the revolts and explored the ways in which this historical moment might be remembered.

Hikayat Meedan re-enacted scenes of the revolution. It was produced by the young Egyptian Artists Group, which began as a Facebook group administered by Amro Qabeel, who became the director of the independent ensemble. The show begins with an old man, once a revolutionary, telling his granddaughter the story of "the Square," referring of course to Tahrir Square. The events of the play take place in a fictional future, and the grandfather tells tales from his past, the audience's present.

As the grandfather narrates, the rest of the performers enact his stories. The play consists of a series of independent but linked scenes, each tackling a unique subject. The grandfather and granddaughter characters tie these scenes together. Each scene revolves around a problem that affects the average Egyptian citizen, such as the difficulty of obtaining bread. Men, women, and children wait for hours in long bread lines until they are exhausted and end up with nothing.

Another scene focuses on illegal migration: a group of young men decide to emigrate in order to find work abroad instead of remaining unemployed in Egypt. Each in turn bids his family farewell. Elderly parents and lovers seeking marriage beg them to stay. The young men leave Egypt, but none of them reaches foreign shores. Their ship sinks, and they drown, their dreams dying with them. The performance also includes songs, some trenchant with critique like "Our Government Has Sold Us," and concludes with a famous patriotic melody to which the audience could sing along.

The production was self-financed by the ensemble members. They performed in a number of sites including the Amir Taz Palace in an old Cairo neighborhood, Saladin Fort Square, Al Salaam Theatre, and Suez City Theatre, among others. Their production elements were simple – they wore plain white, black, and red clothes, the colors of the Egyptian flag, and layered costumes over these as needed.

The second piece, *Kharabeesh*, portrayed the endemic corruption of the Mubarak regime. *Kharabeesh* is an Egyptian word describing the scratch of fingernails on flesh. The play, written by Khamees Ezzalarab and directed by Iman Al Sirfi, was performed by the Youth Theatre, affiliated with the Ministry of Culture, in the Italian Black Box in Cairo. The two-act play follows a ruling family of cats and their mouse subjects – the hunters and the prey. The Ruler Cat, his arrogant feline wife, and their spoiled son oppress the mice, depriving them of employment. While they import rotten food from abroad for their subjects, they indulge themselves in fine cuisine. Their rule is buttressed by the Big Cat, a foreign autocrat donning the stars and stripes of the American flag, who keeps the Ruler Cat under his thumb.

When the mice stage acts of civil disobedience, they are imprisoned. One of the younger, courageous mice sneaks into the palace in disguise and uncovers a conspiracy brewing between the mother cat and her spoiled son, his eye on the throne, against the father. Thus, the show presents a palace rife with corruption and ruled by personal interest with no regard for the people. But the world of symbolism and metaphor unravels when the characters begin to embody actual political personalities, including the former president Hosni Mubarak. This candor destroys the world created by the performance, especially when the actors salute young revolutionaries; reality overpowers the symbolism of the play.

The third piece, outside of Cairo, was *Al Jeel Abu Zalouma*. The show was produced in Port Fuad, one of the cities along the Suez Canal in the Port Said region. These cities are renowned for their history of popular resistance during three critical moments in Egypt's history: the Suez Crisis of 1956, the 1967 War with Israel, and the October War with Israel in 1973. The performance presumed familiarity with this local history. Written by Rajib Salim and directed by Muhammad Hassan, the story follows preparations for the grand opening of a new national museum to commemorate the martyrs of those wars.

The governor and the ruling party leader, who doubles as a well-known businessman and the parliament representative for the museum's district, are expected to attend. But the statues of the martyrs go missing without a trace. The police launch an investigation and summon the daughter of a martyr, a beautiful young woman notorious for being a promiscuous gold-digger. She knows nothing about the stolen statue of her father and does not care. Next, the police summon an unemployed drug addict, the son of a martyr, and he is similarly apathetic.

In the end, the statues reappear and actually spring into life, but they refuse to return to the museum. They claim that the governor and the parliamentarian have used them to manipulate the emotions of the people and further their own material gain. "Did I die so that someone like him can live off my blood?" asks a martyred soldier, pointing to the parliamentarian, a fashionable, well-built man whose appearance bespeaks greed.

These three plays demonstrate some of the ways in which theatre artists have initiated discussions about how and why the revolution occurred. Watching these and other productions, I wondered why these young Egyptians were not satisfied with the virtual world of Facebook, YouTube, and Twitter as venues of dialogue with a much wider audience than at live performances. Perhaps reflecting as a society on our hopes, dreams, pain, and worries requires the immediacy of the theatre, where we come together and exchange not only emotions and opinions but also the very air we breathe.

Based on a translation by Meris Lutz

6

Staging a Protest: Socio-Political Critique in Contemporary Yemeni Theatre

Katherine Hennessey

At this particular historical moment in the Middle East, theatre seems to serve primarily as a metaphor for a dearth of honest consideration of socio-political problems. Comparisons to the theatre abound in descriptions of the negotiations and political posturing provoked by the protests of the Arab Spring, where frequently one side describes the other's actions as "a farce," "a surreal scene," a "black comedy," or, even more dismissively, as "mere theatre."[1] At the same time, various groups of protesters seem to have grasped the potentially transformative power of theatrical performance as the late Syrian playwright Saadallah Wannous understood it.

In the public spaces of the Yemeni capital Sanaa, for example, members of the youth protest movement have performed skits, scenes, and musical interludes to express their anger and desire for political and social change during the uprisings of the Arab Spring. These dramatized dialogues have accompanied performative acts that typically characterize mass protests – speeches to assembled crowds, marches of hundreds and thousands of protestors, chants and gestures performed in unison, and so on. Thus, it seems timely to interrogate the relationships between theatrical performance and socio-political protest and to consider the ways in which theatre may still be effective in provoking critical dialogue within and between communities, the kind of dialogue for which the late Syrian playwright Saadallah Wannous hoped.

Yemen is not well known for contentious or groundbreaking works of theatre; in fact, from outside of Yemen, one would be hard pressed to discover that Yemeni drama even exists. Full-fledged theatrical performances are few, and large-scale productions like the ones discussed in this essay generally occur only through the support of a Western embassy or cultural center. While a vibrant culture of performance certainly exists on the small scale – dramatic monologues performed at wedding celebrations, recitations of poetry, and rhetoric at public and semi-public gatherings – it is quite rare to see a curtain rise on an actual stage.

This has not always been the case. The history of Yemeni theatre stretches back to the first decade of the twentieth century, and perhaps much further.[2] The dramas of Yemen's prolific playwrights chronicle formative historical events in both the North and the South, and these plays have appeared alongside Yemeni performances of Shakespeare, Pirandello, Brecht, and Racine, among others. Every major Yemeni city boasted a local theatre troupe for at least a small part of the twentieth century. And in just four years in the mid 1960s, the television station in Aden, capital of South Yemen (the People's Democratic Republic of Yemen), broadcast live performances of over 200 plays.

More recent decades have not been as kind to the genre. The unification of North and South Yemen in 1990 gave rise to a certain amount of government-sponsored spectacle and pageantry over the course of the subsequent decade, but theatrical performance withered. The plays discussed in this essay constitute what may prove to be a slow but significant return of the theatre to prominence in Yemen, beginning in the early years of the twenty-first century.

The Yemeni government currently does little to foster the performing arts. Lack of financial support is a recurring lament among theatre practitioners in

Yemen, as is the dearth of appropriate performance spaces and of audio-visual technology and equipment. The particular performances that I discuss here all took place in Sanaa at the Markaz Al Thaqafa (the Cultural Center), which is an auditorium rather than a theatre, better suited to official ceremonies and speeches delivered from a podium than to staged performance. It is important to note that the government refrains from taking concrete, targeted steps to hinder theatrical performance and free expression therein. However, government officials may occasionally request to read plays and scripts prior to production, sometimes justifying their interventions in the scripts through a paternalistic logic of "protecting the audience from fright" rather than that of repressing political critique, however implicit.[3]

When, despite the aforementioned obstacles, dramatic performances do take place in Yemen, they attract large and keenly enthusiastic crowds of spectators, who openly manifest their delight with or disapproval of what unfolds before them on the stage – and while there is much to delight, there is also potentially much to offend. In the last few years, a number of playwrights, actors, and actresses have critiqued the ills of contemporary Yemeni society and challenged Yemen's socio-cultural strictures, its time-hallowed *adat wa taqaleed*[4] (customs and traditions), and the rampant corruption they perceive in government and big business. In doing so, they have given dramatic form and embodied expression to criticisms of government and society that, in Yemen prior to the Arab Spring protests, were usually voiced in the confines of much smaller and more intimate gatherings.

This essay examines three works of contemporary Yemeni theatre: *Maak Nazl* (I'll Go With You) by Amr Jamal and the Khaleej Aden theatre troupe, and *The Ravings of Birds that have Lost their Wings* and *Where Are You Now?* by Qasim Abbas Al Lami, Khaled Al Yusufi, and the Future Partners for Development Foundation.[5] The essay explores these plays' critiques of patriarchal, repressive, and regressive elements in Yemeni society, arguing that Yemeni theatre creates a space in which alternative visions of collective

Yemeni identity can be envisioned, embodied, and discussed. As such, the production of these plays in 2009 and 2010 presaged the youth movement's seizing and inhabiting of actual physical space in Yemeni cities, like Change Square in Sanaa in 2011, and that movement's own attempts at performative dialogue with their audience: the government, their fellow Yemenis, and the outside world.

Maak Nazl

A boisterous crowd gathered in the auditorium of the Cultural Center in Sanaa. In keeping with urban Yemeni norms of gender segregation, groups of men took seats on the left side of the large hall while on the right sat women and families. Before the curtain rose, a burly security guard paced through the aisles, making sure that audience members sat in their proper sections, swatting any small boy who stood on the seat cushions. The crowd had gathered to watch a theatre troupe from the southern Yemeni city of Aden perform a musical entitled *Maak Nazl*.

Though set in modern-day Aden, *Maak Nazl* is based on a 1980s cult hit from Berlin's GRIPS Theatre. In the German original, entitled *Linie 1* (Line 1), a naïve young woman from the German countryside travels to the city to find the rock-star boyfriend who has abandoned her. She has a series of epiphanies on the underground train lines[6] in Berlin, where she meets scheming prostitutes, jovial drunks, suicidal drug addicts, mischievous socialites, and formidable widows nostalgic for the era of the Third Reich.

In the Yemeni adaptation by playwright and director Amr Jamal, a young girl from a rural village travels to Aden to find the husband who has deserted her after a "tourist marriage."[7] She has borne him a son in his absence and is desperate to locate him so that, among other things, he can sign the baby's birth certificate and legitimize him. The Young Woman begins her journey through the big city anxious and alone. No one knows the address that she is searching for, the ironically named "Hope Street." But Ahmed, a good-hearted young security guard, shyly offers what help he can, including directions to his blind mother's sandwich shop so that the Young Woman can eat something after her purse is stolen.

As she wanders the city in search of Hope, the Young Woman meets Aden residents from all walks of life, from venerable street-sweepers to vapid students, from a comically mismatched couple about to have their first child to a trio of crotchety old women – played by male actors – nostalgic for Aden's eras of British occupation and Socialism. Even a Somali immigrant and the coterie of friends she calls on her mobile phone form part of the mosaic.[8] As the scenes and characters' stories unfold, the play presents Aden as an ever expanding, heterogeneous imagined community, its members downtrodden but undaunted by their perpetual struggle against a stagnant economy, corrupt bureaucracy, and rigid set of social strictures.

The stories that the other characters share with the Young Woman eventually provoke her to fundamentally re-evaluate her quest. By the final scene, face-to-face with her rich "tourist husband" and his oily assurances that he loves her and that his absence was only meant to be temporary, she realizes that she does not want the life he has promised her, nor does she want her son to have him as a father. She chooses instead to return to the community she has discovered in Aden, where she reunites with the bashful Ahmed to universal rejoicing.

Albeit in comedic fashion, the play critiques many of the ills of contemporary Yemeni society, from the rural poverty that has made the protagonist easy prey for her affluent "tourist husband" to soaring rates of unemployment, from the abject failure of the nation's educational system to entrenched gender-based inequality. From the first scene onwards, the play pillories the Yemeni government and the country's wealthy elite when Ahmed convinces an assembled crowd not to press charges against the town drunk[9] when the latter bungles an attempt at pickpocketing:

> Ahmed: Besides, the whole country steals. We're furious with this wretch, but what's he next to the professional thieves who steal the country's resources?
> Awood: From that perspective, what you're saying seems reasonable, officer.[10]

The play also challenges Yemeni norms of gendered behavior on multiple levels, first and foremost by taking the emotions and intellectual growth of a young and unchaperoned female as its primary focus. The Young Woman begins the play seeking protection and direction in the form of a male figure, her "tourist husband." When intimidated by other characters, she invents an uncle who is "as strong as an ox and on his way to meet her."[11] By the play's conclusion, however, she has grown sufficiently strong and self-aware to reject the socially sanctioned option of attempting to make a life with the father of her child. Ahmed also makes a choice that some Yemeni men would find unthinkable: he is prepared to marry a young woman who was duped and abandoned by another man and to raise that man's child as his own.

Maak Nazl effectively inverts class distinctions as well. The play's only wealthy character is the Young Woman's absentee husband, whose ethical flaws are obvious. A more striking reversal of expectations arises in the portrayal of the poorest character, the elderly street-sweeper. In Yemen, those who sweep the streets form part of the often isolated and disdained underclass known as the *akhdam* (servants), yet in the play, the street-sweeper is the first character to show kindness and concern for the Young Woman. He is also confident enough in his own wisdom and experience of the world to berate egocentric teenagers Rami and Akram for skipping school to feed their PlayStation obsession at the local video store.

By advertising the play in the major Yemeni papers and spreading the word on the street,[12] as well as by providing free admission, the production succeeded in attracting an audience that mirrored the heterogeneous group shown on the stage. Members of Yemen's intellectual and artistic elite – from ministers and politicians to much-admired actor Nabeel Hizam – rubbed shoulders with Yemenis of much lower social status. Many in the audience audibly identified with the lower-class characters: a large swathe of spectators joined in when the street-sweeper began to sing a familiar melody, and by the final performance almost the entire audience chimed in with the alcoholic character's tag line: "I'm not drunk ... I'm just *drinking*!"[13] Much of the audience seemed, in fact, to want to participate in the community portrayed on the stage.

The Ravings of Birds that have Lost their Wings

Ravings and *Where Are You Now?*, each in one act and performed in sequence, are works of experimental theatre and remarkably distinct both verbally and visually from *Maak Nazl*. *Ravings* features a series of actresses who vividly describe the oppressive role that fathers and other male figures have played in their lives, reliving memories of physical and psychological abuse, indifference, and abandonment and candidly exploring the depths and ambivalence of the resultant emotions. The play opens and closes with a dance sequence, which bookends six vignettes. Five of the vignettes take the form of soliloquies delivered by the female cast members and directed towards an absent male: the Father, the Lover, the Brother, the Religious Leader, and the Stepfather.

The script, as its prefatory note explains, arose through a collaborative effort. Director Qasim Abbas Al Lami and the acting troupe had chosen Yemeni women's rights as their theme.[14] In a discussion of "the reality of

Yemeni women's lives," many of the troupe's actresses complained of men's coercive influence. The group thus decided to envision a city in which the men had died and to imagine what the surviving women might then be free to say to the departed males.

"The Father" is the first soliloquy. Bending over a coffin, actresses Manal Al Mulaiki and Rua[15] open the scene:[16]

> Rua: Oh, Father ... You don't know how the sound of
> your voice terrified me.
> Manal: I dreaded the sight of your face, dreaded it.

While Manal recounts her youthful dreams of fatherly affection, Rua explains the bitter reality: the Father's violence towards her mother pushes their house into a "state of emergency," with all of the physical and psychological damage that such a state implies. In a spare but compelling dozen lines, the two women describe years of enduring the Father's quotidian oppression. They end the scene by raining curses upon the Father's corpse:

> Manal: Die, Father, die!
> Rua: Die from all of your ugliness—
> Manal: And your injustice—
> Rua: And your tyranny—
> Both: Die ... die ... die!

The Stepfather (called "The Mother's Husband" in the script), who beats his stepdaughter, ignoring the pitiful pleas of her wheelchair-bound mother, receives an equally ferocious postmortem denunciation. His stepdaughter Saba[17] avers that he has destroyed both her life and her mother's through his physical and verbal violence:

> Saba: I don't believe you're even human. I don't believe you have a heart capable of mercy or compassion. In my whole life with you, I've met with nothing but violence and beatings and insults and abuse, and for no reason. And not just me, but my poor mother, too.

The helplessness of mothers to defend their daughters (and vice versa) from male violence is a recurring theme, as is the irrational nature of that violence and its utter lack of justification. It is perhaps for this reason that the play reserves its most visceral condemnation for the spiritual father, the "Man of Religion." Instead of espousing precepts of love, mercy, and self-discipline, the Man of Religion embodies bigotry, hypocrisy, and fanaticism. He has died, Manal informs us, because after long years spent poisoning others' lives, his body "could no longer endure its own venom."[18] Rua and Manal revile him – "Curse you, curse you a thousand times" – and rejoice at the relief that his last breath will bring to those around him: "Die, for your death will bring life to me and to other men and women."[19]

Yet although the play defines certain forms of male domination as unjust and tyrannical, it does not present the male sex as uniformly oppressive. In stark contrast to her excoriation of "the Father," Manal alludes to her father with love and respect when she plays a different character.[20] One female character recounts ambiguous feelings towards her deceased beloved; despite their conflicts and her jealousy while he was alive, she laments his death.[21] And in the final scene, while tending to her much-loved father's grave, a character discovers in her suitor a man who promises to always respect her as a human being.[22]

The dance sequences also provide a distancing effect, a salutary reminder that the audience is in fact watching actresses playing roles that should be viewed as more symbolic than singular. Each woman holds a huge wooden rectangle mounted on tiny wheels, an enormous picture frame. The dance, as the women alternately drag the frames across the stage, posing, stepping, riding, and whirling around them, visually implies various messages: that Yemeni women are more than objects to be gazed upon; that many feel confined by the rigid boundaries placed upon and around them; and that the complexities of human experience cannot be contained in a simple frame – just as they cannot be reduced to a dramatic soliloquy, however powerful.

Even the play's title suggests that the soliloquies are expressions of extreme emotion rather than descriptions of reality: the word that I have translated as "ravings" has a range of meanings from "drivel" to "delirium" to "hallucinations."[23] As such, the ferocious anger expressed in some of the lines could be seen as a momentary reaction to a shocking and unexpected loss rather than a full-throated rejection of patriarchal authority.

Despite these internal attempts to temper the critique, there is no doubt that, to a Yemeni audience, *Ravings* presents a stunning denunciation of male oppression; the representation of more sensitive and more compassionate men is simply overshadowed by the unexpected spectacle of daughters cursing their father and women verbally eviscerating their imam. As a member of the audience for a performance in the spring of 2010, I watched and admired the courage of the actresses as they performed with fierce conviction. Some of the audience members responded similarly; others did not. A deputy minister from the Yemeni government urgently insisted to me during the interval that Yemeni women would never actually say the things that I was hearing onstage. "Die, Father?" she repeated incredulously. "No, never. Yemeni women respect their fathers. This could never be said in real life." And yet this *was* said, onstage, in the full view and hearing of hundreds of spectators.

Where Are You Now?

Where Are You Now?, performed by the same troupe and directed by Khaled Al Yusufi, portrays the longing of a young man for the love of his life, and for his friends and his favorite haunts, after all are destroyed in a horrific act of violence. The opening street scene shows Yemenis going about their daily lives: children playing, couples strolling through the park, friends chatting over drinks bought at a soda vendor's cart. The protagonist notices a beautiful young woman wearing a traditional Sanaani dress. A silent courtship begins, in which she shyly returns the protagonist's interest.

A thunderous explosion is heard, and the stage goes dark. When the stage lights come back on, the benches and trees have been overturned; debris is scattered in all directions; and the protagonist finds himself alone amidst the destruction. His shock and confusion are slowly transmuted into grief and nostalgia as he discovers, one by one, the personal possessions of the deceased in the piles of rubble surrounding him. As he picks up a child's ball, for example, the children reappear in a vision and run across the stage playing their game. When he finds a scrap of the Sanaani dress, the young woman appears to him, dressed in ghostly white. She takes his hands, and they slowly dance across the stage before she, too, disappears.

The play contains no dialogue, no lines except for a single phrase spoken by the protagonist to his departed beloved: "Where are you now?" Gestures and facial expressions communicate all of the emotions, from innocent delight to confusion and horror, sadness and longing.

Yet even without words *Where Are You Now?* sparked controversy. The dance sequence, for example, transgressed an obvious gender boundary in Yemen by showing an unrelated man and woman holding hands and dancing together and received derisory whistles and hisses from several members of the audience. The fact that the young woman in her ghostly reappearance wore a headscarf, which revealed much of her hair, added to the perceived affront to accepted standards of Yemeni behavior and female modesty.

The reaction of these audience members may not be an entirely straightforward commentary on what they were watching at that particular moment, however. At least two additional layers of complexity should be noted. Firstly, the woman cast for *Where Are You Now?* also played roles in *Ravings*. The protagonist's beloved young woman was played by Manal Al Mulaiki, who delivered two of the harshest condemnations of patriarchy in the previous play. A negative reaction to her gestures and appearance in the second play may have been compounded by uncomfortable memories of her words in the first.

Secondly, these two plays were financially supported by the American Embassy and were prefaced with a speech by the American ambassador to Yemen.[24] As the performance had been scheduled to coincide with International Human Rights Day, the ambassador welcomed the Future Partners for Development Foundation's interest in human rights issues and assured the audience that the US staunchly supports Yemenis' access to fundamental human rights, among which he cited the right to education, decent health care, and women's rights. The Ambassador's speech may have predisposed some members of the audience to interpret the content of the plays as a covert American critique of Yemeni society and/or of the Yemeni government.

Many Yemenis view US influence on their internal affairs with suspicion. Even some of those who might agree with the content of the critique would do so with less enthusiasm if they suspected that the theatre troupe was being used as a tool to advance an American agenda. The staging of *Where Are You Now?*, portraying the emotional ramifications of a cataclysmic explosion that killed innocent people, coincided temporally with an upsurge in international news coverage about terrorism in Yemen: allegations were circulating that Umar Farouk Abdulmutallib had received training from Al Qaeda extremists based in Yemen for his attempted "underwear bombing" of a Detroit-bound airliner three months prior to the play's performance. It is therefore possible that some members of the audience perceived the choice of theme as influenced by American concerns, and thus interpreted the acts that transgressed Yemeni gender boundaries as a product of foreign influence instead of an indigenous social critique (which might have been marginally more palatable).

Maak Nazl also had outside support from Das Deutsche Haus (a Yemeni-German Cultural Centre, with branches in Sanaa and Aden). The director of the centre, Dr. Guido Zebisch, suggested the project of adapting *Linie 1* to Amr Jamal, whose theatre troupe Khaleej Aden had already staged three highly successful productions in Aden. Das Deutsche Haus provided financial support; they also contacted the German author Ludwig Voelker for permission and arranged the use of the original musical score. As with the US Embassy's support of the double bill, however, creative control remained in the hands of the director and the actors.[25]

In addition to foreign sponsorship, Jamal and the Khaleej Aden actors' base in the south of Yemen also, ironically, makes them "outsiders" in Sanaa. The theatre troupe hails from the epicenter of the southern separatist movement, which calls for dissolution of the 1990 unification. This movement began in 2007 and had successfully organized a number of mass demonstrations in Aden and other southern cities by the time of the play's production in 2009. *Maak Nazl*'s critique of "professional thieves who steal the country's resources" channels southern separatists' most consistent complaint: that the Sanaa-based government siphons off the wealth of the South and inequitably "redistributes" it to the North – or worse, simply pockets it.

Furthermore, the Young Woman's rejection of her wealthy but unscrupulous husband in favor of Ahmed is open to interpretation as an allegory for many southern Yemenis' desire to dissolve the union with the North. That her quest centers around a desire to legitimize her child and thereby ensure him a secure future, while her "husband" tries to avoid that responsibility altogether, seems an obvious indictment of the post-unification government – a message that could have offended at least some members of a Sanaa audience.

Yet overall, the audience's response to the performance of *Maak Nazl* in Sanaa was unabashedly enthusiastic. Though the same cannot be said for *Ravings* and *Where Are You Now?*, it should be noted that the content of all three plays seemed to generate a similarly intense level of interest and engagement on the part of the audience.

* * *

It is remarkable to think that *Maak Nazl*, *Ravings*, and *Where Are You Now?* were staged in Sanaa well before any hint of the Arab Spring had appeared there. After all, the protests in Yemen – with their carefully choreographed chants, symbolic mass gestures, improvised street performances, ironic humor, and courageous denunciations of a corrupt regime – contain striking parallels to all these plays. This is not to imply, of course, any causal connection between the performance of *Maak Nazl* and Arab Spring protests in Yemen,[26] but merely to point out that, in their theatricality and their freedom of expression as well as in certain of their thematics, the youth protests on the streets of Yemen in 2011 mirror various aspects of the theatrical performances that took place in 2009 and 2010.

The protest movement echoes at least two of the fundamental motifs in the double bill and *Maak Nazl*, respectively: (a) the fierce anger and profound sadness of many ordinary Yemenis at the conditions in which their country now finds itself, which they attribute to corruption and irresponsibility within the current regime; and (b) the belief that citizens' words and actions can change the current political state and actually create a new and different kind of community. If theatre had flourished in Yemen over the past 20 years to the same extent that it has in the last three, perhaps the changes called for by today's youth protestors on the streets of Yemen's cities might have been more easily effectuated, or at least more thoroughly debated.

As things stand, the dialogue that Wannous suggested could take place inside the theatre has moved, in many ways, to those streets. But the current stalemate in Yemen seems to suggest that no one is willing to play the role of audience – to entertain, even momentarily, the other side's perspective. Thus no meaningful dialogue can take place, and no transcendent new sense of national community can arise. Perhaps partisans from all sides should turn their attention back to the potential of the theatre. For whether audience members applaud or criticize what they see on stage, whether they sing along with or protest what they hear, the three works of Yemeni theatre treated here do provide some hope that dialogue is still possible.

Notes

1. For one recent example among many, see Duraid Al Baik's "Syria Opens Two-Day National Dialogue," *Gulf News*, Dubai, July 11, 2011.
2. Some Yemeni scholars contend that the first Yemeni play was Sheikh Faqih Abdullah Ibn Omar Ba Makhrama's *Dialogue Between Hadramout and Her Son*, written in the sixteenth century; others have posited that the ancient Yemeni kingdoms of Sheba, Himyar, and Qataban all had forms of theatre. For discussions of this and of the rich heritage of Yemeni drama more generally, see, for example, Said Al Aulaqi, *Sabaun Aaman min al-Masrah fi al-Yemen* [Seven Years of Theatre in Yemen] (Aden: Directorate of Publications, Ministry of Culture and Tourism, People's Democratic Republic of Yemen, 1983); Yahya Muhammad Sayf, *al-Mukhtasar al-Mufid fi al-Masrah al-Arabi al-Jadid: al-Masrah fi al-Yemen* [Critical Digest of New Arab Theatre: Theatre in Yemen] (Sharjah: Secretariat-General for Arab Theatre, 2009).
3. For example, Mr. Guido Zebisch, director of the German House for Cooperation and Culture in Yemen, recounted to me that the script of *Maak Nazl* had been

read prior to performance by a government official. He requested the omission of one small section in which characters joked that the extinct volcano was going to erupt. A neighborhood in Aden known as "Crater" is named after this extinct volcano. The official apparently explained that he was concerned this could cause members of the audience to panic. Interview by the author, Sanaa, January 27, 2010. Government censors may also request to read scripts in order to ensure that they contain no attacks on Islam, the Prophet, or any government officials who are actually named.

4. In Yemen, this phrase carries allusions to conservative social practices based on tribal norms.
5. All three plays are currently unpublished. I am grateful to Guido Zebisch and Ahmed Al Asery for providing me with copies of the scripts. It should be noted that these are working copies rather than finalized texts, and that in some places the scripts have been subject to additions and improvisations by the cast members. The lines that I quote below were delivered essentially verbatim in the performances that I attended.
6. As the city of Aden does not have an underground rail system, the Young Woman's peregrinations take place via the microbus system found in Yemeni cities, a transportation network which the play references as a symbol for the "journey of life" undertaken by its various characters. In fact, the play's title literally means "I'll descend/get down with you," with "from the bus" being implied.
7. A euphemism used in Yemen for the phenomenon of wealthy Gulf Cooperation Council citizens who travel to Yemen and marry young Yemeni women, having promised them lives of ease and luxury, then disappear after their honeymoon.
8. Immigrants and refugees from the Horn of Africa often live on the socio-economic, as well as geographic, margins of Yemeni society. I should note that the scene featuring the Somali woman, also played by a male cast member, does not appear in the official text of the play but was a crowd-pleasing addition to performance.
9. *Maak Nazl* is also notable for its honest though comic treatment of alcohol abuse in Yemen.
10. Amr Jamal, "Maak Nazl" (unpublished playscript, 2009), 2. English translations by the author.
11. Ibid., 2.
12. The organizers hired cars equipped with megaphone systems to drive through the labyrinthine lanes of the capital, announcing the performance via loudspeaker.

13. It was astonishing to hear the glee with which hundreds of Yemenis chanted this line, perhaps an indication of relief, by some members of the audience at least, at being able to admit, aloud and in public, to drinking alcohol despite the Islamic prohibition.
14. Qasim Abbas Al Lami et al., "Ravings of Birds that have Lost their Wings" (unpublished playscript, 2010), 2. The performance coincided with International Human Rights Day as well as International Theatre Day.
15. An established actress on Yemeni television as well as the stage, Rua is listed in the script only by her first name.
16. Though their lines are complementary, with one actress occasionally completing or expounding upon what has just been expressed by the other, it appeared in performance that the two women are not supposed to play the roles of sisters but rather to be two unrelated women, each of whom has endured a similar form of paternal oppression.
17. Played by actress and poet Saba Al Awadi. The script gives all of the characters the name of the actress or actor who plays them.
18. Al Lami, "Ravings," 5.
19. Ibid.
20. "Oh, how I love you, Father ..." Al Lami, "Ravings," 5.
21. "I so much wanted you to be near me ... but I don't wish for that anymore. Now I wish for you to be far, far away, on one condition: that you be alive ... safe and sound." Al Lami, "Ravings," 4.
22. Ibid., 8.
23. Hans Wehr, *Dictionary of Modern Written Arabic*, 4th edn., ed. J. Milton Cowan (Urbana, IL: Spoken Language Services, 1994).
24. The fact that Stephen Seche, American ambassador to Yemen at the time, had arranged to make a rare appearance at this very public function would have been sufficient to mark the evening as uncommon, but the ambassador even took to the podium to welcome the audience in Arabic. Afterwards, he delivered his remarks to the assembled spectators in English, translated in sequence.
25. Zebisch describes the role of Das Deutsche Haus in the play's production as simply creating a space in which Jamal and the actors could express their views, concerns, and talents; neither he nor anyone else from the Cultural Center intervened to shape or censor the content. Zebisch, interview. The production took place as part of a public celebration of the 40th anniversary of the re-establishment of German-Yemeni diplomatic relations.
26. At the time of writing (September 2011), governmental, opposition, tribal, extremist, and other factions are vying for political control over various parts

of Yemen. For the purposes of this essay, however, the "Arab Spring protests in Yemen" refer only to the youth movement which began in late January 2011 in the wake of the Tunisian uprising, coalescing in February 2011 at the entrance of Sanaa University (i.e. Change Square) in Sanaa, as well as in other Yemeni cities. The movement captured the initial spirit of awakening and change pervading the Middle East at the time. Like the southern separatist movement, the youth protests continue.

7

The Legacy of Saadallah Wannous and *Soirée for the 5th of June* amidst the Arab Revolts

Asaad Al-Saleh

In the summer of 2011, the Syrian Minister of Culture canceled the final showcase performance by graduating students of the High Institute of Dramatic Arts in Damascus due to the unfolding events in Syria. Renowned actor Fayez Qazaq, who directed the student production, commented on the decision in the press by asking, "Where is [Saadallah] Wannous, whose work was banned even after he died and is absent from the Syrian stage, for reasons that are all too suspicious? Why? Where is his legacy?"[1] In turn, one could question the revival of Wannous's memory 15 years after his death. Is it because Wannous was subjected to the same oppression under which the current generation of Syrian dramatists suffers, or is it because the regime wishes for his contributions to disappear and be forgotten? The events in Syria since March 15, 2011, when uprisings consolidated into a national revolt, confirm that Wannous's theatrical conceptions of tyranny and its restrictions on freedom remain relevant to what is happening today.

With the onset of authoritarianism, dialogue vanished in Syria decades ago. Wannous lamented this state of affairs and the lack of dialogue in contemporary Arab society: "We are not trained in dialogue, nor do we appreciate the significance of diversity, debate, or fulfilling our freedom.

Our lives are like two monologues, one official and oppressive, and the other popular and oppressed."[2] For Wannous, a plurality of voices and the inevitable contradictions that arise therein create a dialectical space similar to the one discussed by literary theorist Mikhail Bakhtin, whose views on the novel as an art of pluralistic voices Wannous has credited as an intellectual influence.[3] The 1960s, during which Wannous wrote *Soirée for the 5th of June* (1968), witnessed not only the external defeat of Arab armies at the hands of Israel but also the internal homogenization of voices. The motto "no voice is louder than the sound of the battle" suffused the nation, rendering the entire country a military zone where commands were issued and the people no longer had any say.

At this stage and for a number of reasons, including his attempt to avoid direct confrontation with the regime, Wannous took refuge in heritage[4] and used it to address political reality. In his play *The Adventures of Jabr the Mamluk's Head* (1970), he uses the *hakawati*, or storyteller, and the modern cafe to show how the regime pursues a particular agenda of special interests that are not only bad for the country but may even bring about its destruction. In the play, which interweaves events and characters from thirteenth-century Iraq, the people of Baghdad are passive, and consequently the self-interested Caliph is able to monopolize control. Given the acquiescence of the people and the Caliph's neglect, Baghdad easily falls to the hands of an invading foreign enemy.

Wannous's work is always critical of despots, but he also holds the people accountable for maintaining socio-political awareness and for taking action. In his play *The King is King* (1977), the ruler is creative in his humiliation of the people, replacing himself on the throne with Abu Azza the Idiot because he has grown bored. In order to highlight the depth of the gap between the ruler and the people, Wannous creates a political world that revolves around those at the center of power. They rule the country and loot the people's livelihood while the people are expected to welcome their controllers. Syrian intellectual and opposition activist Abdel Razzaq Eid saw in this play "an implicit parody targeting those generals who led the volatile political history of Syria."[5] Wannous creates artistic spaces using political and historical events to expose the ruling authority and its mentality, which do not satisfy the interests and aspirations of the citizens. Thus, all of Wannous's political plays can by analyzed within the framework of this need to communicate, in the present and future, the ways in which people are robbed of agency while the ruling authority enjoys absolute power.

Wannous was among the first Arab writers in Syria to call for dialogue from a political standpoint with the intention of enacting change. His theatre was open to public engagement and aimed to be democratic in the sense that he shared with his audience the mechanics and implications of the action unfolding on the stage. In "Manifestos for a New Arab Theatre," Wannous wrote that theatre has been and remains political, "even when it appears indifferent to politics and avoids its problems."[6] Theatre, in his view, is also a social phenomenon rooted in the public's problems; it engages these issues without presenting a final solution: "We make theatre because we want to change and develop a mentality and deepen the collective awareness of our shared historical destiny."[7] Although Bertolt Brecht, one of his intellectual influences, did not believe that theatre was capable of "achieving revolution" or "altering the structure of society,"[8] Wannous understood by studying his society that revolution against the establishment was inevitable, especially if the ruling authority slammed the door in the face of dialogue, as happens in *Soirée for the 5th of June*. There are challenges to dialogue, and Wannous used what was available to him to overcome these challenges and do away with fear and blind dependency. Wannous, who was committed to a political, humanitarian cause, could find no regime representative willing to speak with him; engaging in dialogue with intellectuals was not considered an option for the regime, and it remains a rare, if improbable, practice.

Wannous turns to dialogue despite the insistence by government officials that contemporaneous political events in the 1960s can be blamed on an internationally coordinated enemy. In the words of the character of the director in *Soirée*, who is an opponent of democratic dialogue, the events are "a total conspiracy, and I would not rule out the presence of foreign powers behind [them],"[9] who are also responsible for "stirring up matters that harm the security and general welfare of the state" (131). Wannous tried to open a dialogue at a time in the Arab world when dialogue was not expected to solve problems or reveal the people behind those problems. At the time, the hegemonic discourse shaped "the other" into an enemy that must be uprooted without hesitation, without considering that the defeat of 1967 may have been a result of internal weakness. In *Rape* (1990), Wannous writes himself into the play as the character "Saadallah," and "Saadallah" agrees to speak with an Israeli doctor, who turns out to be more human than the image depicted by the machinery of the regime. In 1967, the government had championed slogans of resistance right up until it took the unilateral decision, without consulting its citizens, to negotiate with Israeli politicians like Yitzhak Rabin, one of the masterminds of the 1967 War. The character "Saadallah" asks the doctor: "Do you think you and I can live with [Golda] Meir, Gideon [Hausner], and [Moshe] Dayan?"[10] To this day, the question remains unanswered, one of the reasons why Wannous and his play have sparked such a controversy.

Wannous wrote his first play, *Life Forever*, in 1961. According to Wannous expert Marie Elias, his first work revolves around the humanist idea that "the life force cannot be overridden by other forces; it always emerges victorious."[11] Perhaps Wannous foresaw that the end of his own humanist journey – the last years of his life from 1992 to 1996 – would be a struggle for survival and a challenge against the idea of death. This foresight can also be seen in the events anticipated by Wannous in *Soirée*, as he insists that the people will not remain silent, that they will revolt. His early works also indicate that Wannous had drawn for himself a clear path dedicated to exposing the tyranny of the ruling powers and drawing attention to the gulf that separates the ruling powers from the people. "I know their thoughts and intentions, and I grab them by their leash so that they do not escape,"[12] says the ruler to his daughter Hera in *Medusa Staring at Life*, which Wannous wrote in 1963. Using his pen, the playwright strips away all of the masks that hide the tyrant clinging to power even when corruption and incompetence spread through his regime. Wannous's political plays reflect on how a ruler or official representative becomes a force of the citizen's oppression, a theme which transcends the specifics of time and place to include the political structure of Arab society as a whole.

The play *Soirée* falls within what critics consider the second dramaturgical phase[13] of Wannous's career, a phase which also includes *The Elephant, the King of All Time* (1969), *The Adventures of Jabr the Mamluk's Head* (1970), and *An Evening with Abi Khalil Al Qabbani* (1972). The defeat in 1967 serves as the historical and political starting point for this period, which changed the critical orientation of many Arab writers and artists. But unlike other writers who also addressed the defeat, Wannous utilized theatre as a creative political tool, making him a pioneer among his peers at the time and later when he revisited the subject. His approach during this period was influenced by world theatre and liberation movements of the 1960s. Wannous had gone on an academic trip to France in 1966, which he followed with a series of similar trips, returning at the end of 1968. Thus, he wrote *Soirée* at the peak of his intellectual and artistic maturity, which coincided with the June 1967 defeat. Well versed in European theatre culture and deeply affected by the reality of an Arab world reeling from defeat, Wannous asked: why have we been defeated, and who is responsible?

Lost Freedom

When Wannous was asked in 1986 why he had not written a new play since *The King is King* in 1977, he replied that theatre "cannot be made unless its primary demand is realized, and that demand is freedom."[14] Theatre historian Mohammad Ismail Bassal attributes the creative explosion which took place in Wannous's final years to his physical and existential struggle, "when death began a dialogue with him ... and there was nothing in this world that could stop his mind."[15] Does this imply that fear for oneself is the primary impediment to free thought, and if it disappears, that the artist or intellectual is able to reveal the secrets of his creativity free of restrictions? Despite winning an award from UNESCO and the Syrian Ministry of Culture's first award for theatre in 1968, *Soirée* was banned from publication by the very same ministry, even as it was nominated to be included in the National Theatre's 1969 season.[16] It was first performed in Beirut in early 1970, the same year it was nominated, and then rejected, to be part of the Damascus Performing Arts Festival. In fact, the play was not performed in Syria until 1973.

The writers of Wannous's generation lived in a grim reality characterized by the loss of liberty. In his era, the barriers to freedom were not the result of Western colonialism or Ottoman imperialism but rather oppressive regimes run by a few compatriots. This reality of oppression clashed with the post-independence "nationalist project" called for by writers and intellectuals in the 1960s. That project consisted of a plan to work towards the future and "change the reality, liberate the land politically and economically, and achieve social justice" – goals which, according to cultural historian Hassan Attiyeh, included raising "nationalist self-awareness on both the cultural and historical levels."[17] By the Arab Spring of 2011, this nationalist project had still not been realized, neither by the people nor by the government, due to the same authoritarian obstacles faced by Wannous, especially in the early part of his career.

Wannous is known for experimenting with theatre as a tool for instigating change against the regime. His early works rely on a discourse similar to his later plays but use it to expose authority and strip away its masked ruthlessness, an approach that characterizes *The Tragedy of the Poor Molasses Vendor* (1964) and *The King is King* (1977). This early phase is marked by experimentation and inspired by local performance heritage, which Wannous projects onto his contemporary reality, his primary focus. As far as Wannous is concerned, experimentation "proves the [necessity] of research and diligence to the complete theater process."[18] The political events of 1967 reinforced his intellectual view of social reality and the means to change it through theatre, making him, as he said to those in his close circle, truly committed to what he wrote, more than simply a producer of texts. According to the late novelist Abdel Rahman Munif and Palestinian literary critic Faisal Darraj, he embodied a link between culture and values, emphasizing that "an intellectual's thoughts are equal to his deeds."[19]

Lost freedom was one of Wannous's primary concerns; he recreated freedom in the artistic sphere while pushing to make it accessible despite the efforts of the authorities to pounce on any demands and terminate debate through suppression and abuse, as we see in the production history of *Soirée*. But Wannous, who embraced Marxist thought, realized that history would witness the end of the regime's tyranny when the people liberated themselves from fear and rose up against it.

Dialogue

What does dialogue mean? For the great physicist and twentieth-century thinker David Bohm, there is a difference between the delivery of an idea or information, merely announcing it, and the dialogue shared by two people that yields something new, a creative process that forms a "link that brings people and communities together."[20] This definition of dialogue in Mikhail Bakhtin's hands becomes linked to human consciousness, providing the only accurate model for expressing authentic human existence. For Bakhtin, "Life is, by nature, interactive, meaning that to live, we must participate in dialogue; we must ask questions, be interested, respond, agree, and so forth."[21]

This humanist understanding of dialogue is intensely present in *Soirée for the 5th of June*, which I would argue exceeds the dimensions of what literary scholar Faten Ali Ammar calls the "authentic nationalism" of theatre; it does more than just "express the wrath of the Arab people" or "expose the defeats of the reactionary military regimes."[22] Wannous wrote it in France, when he was most receptive to the humanist ideas of European theatre. This experience made him realize that the theme of absurdity, which reigned over some spheres of European theatre at that time, like those of Samuel Beckett, comes out of human skepticism in the face of an existence that the mind cannot grasp.

The dialogue in *Soirée* constitutes the artistic structure of the play, which Wannous wanted to be a "live, improvised celebration."[23] The play may be a read as a search for truth in the wake of the 1967 defeat. The questions that drive the play include the following: what really happened? Who is responsible for the defeat? And in what ways have the authorities justified their ongoing failures? In the introduction of the play, Wannous writes that the Israeli attack has revealed "our need to see ourselves, to look in the mirror and ask: who are we, and why?" (5) This mirror and this question determine the intellectual and artistic direction of the play. The play has no breaks and consists of a single textual unit comprised of dense yet sleek dialogue in which, as the subtitle of *Soirée* states, "the audience, history, and officials participate in addition to professional actors."

In the play, the "director," who represents the government, tries to pacify the audience by apologizing for a long delay in the scheduled performance of the play-within-the-play, *The Murmur of Ghosts*. The "playwright," Abd Al Ghani, has let him down by failing to hand over the script. Then, the playwright himself, the "real" Abd Al Ghani, enters the theatre to explain his point of view directly to the audience.

Soirée then turns to the story of a village during and after an attack that leaves the people of the village divided. Some of them call for abandoning the village because they are unable to resist while others prefer resistance. The play employs this story about confused villagers as a political allegory about what happened in the occupied Syrian territories. While the "director" tries to invent victories to attribute to the regime, the troupe reveals the government's failure and its responsibility for the defeat. A heated discussion ensues between the two parties, and "Spectators," characters whom Wannous places throughout the audience, begin to participate in the dialogue and intervene in the action, forcing the reader or actual audience member to rethink the supposed truth of the events, which has been presented by the official narrative in such a way as to serve those responsible for the defeat. Wannous's characters engage in a heated discussion about the consequences of opposing the regime:

> Spectator One: Why have we cut off our tongues?
> Spectator Two: We have not cut off our tongues. Never forget the national interest: a prison of no sunlight, not even once a year. (115)

The pace of the dialogue between the spectators quickens, echoing Wannous's political agitation. When the "director" attempts to stymie talk of freedom, the spectators continue:

> The Group of Spectators: We have not plugged our ears. Never forget the national interest: a prison of no sunlight, not even once a year. (116)

Here, the "Spectators" realize that, until this moment, they have been among the "millions" of plugged ears. The "group of spectators," and perhaps actual audience members, begins participating in the dialogue, responding with their own opinions of the state's rhetoric.

> Spectators: (*from throughout the theatre*) It's all lies. It's all nonsense. It's all drivel. (116)

Through these conversations, Wannous is trying to deepen people's awareness, to make them realize the truth behind the rhetoric that suffuses national and public discourse. As an intellectual, he helps to enable his readers and audience to analyze the regime's rhetoric and respond to it without falling into its trap of nationalist slogans, threats, and accusations of treachery. The search for truth thus unfolds through dialogue. Bakhtin explains this connection: "Truth is not born or present in the mind of one person; rather, it is born among people who collectively search for truth by the process of dialectic interaction amongst themselves."[24] The play is critical of the authorities even as it includes and considers the perspective of the regime, conveyed by the "director." *Soirée*, however, ends in repression when an official "Regime Representative" rises from the front row of the audience. His "henchmen" lock down the theatre and effectively shut down the performance.

After the 1967 defeat, Wannous began intensifying his texts to "testify to the collapse of reality and take direct oppositional action to alter this reality. More precisely, [he] aspired to accomplish the 'active word,' which goes hand in hand with both the dream of revolution and revolutionary action."[25] He tries to artistically tie together words and action by giving the character

"Spectator One" space in *Soirée* to express his opinion with revolutionary enthusiasm and criticize passivity, saying, "Yes, that's me, one of those who read theoretical books on revolutions and peoples, one of those who ruminate on rosy dreams ... I am their escape, you are their escape, we are their escape ... I attack myself in the mirror, I touch my shame in the mirror ... but we are responsible; no one can hide from responsibility" (100).

But how is this responsibility formed? It is a vision of oneself that is stripped of the artificial façade created in official circles. In the play, the mirror becomes a metaphorical tool; gazing into it simply reveals more masks. It helps create an internal dialogue among the audience in the play as if the meeting of two images is equivalent to the meeting of words, of text, in the dialogue. In order to get a clearer picture of what is happening on the political and social front, two audience member characters draw a rectangular mirror and gaze into it but see nothing. "Because we are erased images," Spectator Two explains, "images that were erased by the national interest before they had fully formed" (115).

"National interest" is the discourse used by the state to marginalize the citizen: the national interest supersedes the interests of the individual, and the nation's honor comes before that of the citizen. This is an aspect of the official discourse discussed by political scientist and scholar Lisa Wedeen in her book, *Ambiguities of Domination: Politics, Rhetoric, and Symbols in Contemporary Syria*.[26] Wannous exposed the system of this discourse before it was fully crystallized under former president Hafez Al Assad, after which it became untouchable as a discussion topic.

The intellectual, in Wannous's view, is not someone who sides with the regime and distorts facts for the audience, as does the "director" in his play, calling for music to drown out the calls for freedom and exclaiming: "We will be complicit in this rebellion if we do not put a stop to it" (120). Edward Said defines the intellectual as an individual endowed with a natural ability or power for

> representing, embodying, articulating a message, a view, an attitude, philosophy or opinion to, as well as for, a public ... [someone] whose place it is publicly to raise embarrassing questions, to confront orthodoxy and dogma (rather than to produce them), to be someone who cannot easily be co-opted by governments or corporations and whose raison d'être is to represent all those people and issues that are routinely forgotten.[27]

Wannous uses theatre to convey his cultural, enlightening message indirectly by placing the regime under the gaze of the audience. In this way, the regime's power cannot overcome the power of art and culture, which incite thought to win the battle and stir people to action.

Conclusion

Wannous's dialogue not only presents facts but also tries to "achieve perfect harmony between the stage and the audience."[28] In *Soirée,* this harmony can be seen in the smoothness and dynamism of the dialogue. Wannous wanted his characters to be free of readymade tropes, and so he did away with the traditional structures of playwriting and made room for improvisation. Peasants, intellectuals, and soldiers begin debating among themselves until, eventually, their voices reach the representatives of power. At the end of the play, the regime disperses this democratic assembly, resorting to force and the regurgitated phrases that resemble the vocabulary of contemporary national discourse:

> The Government Official: My countrymen, steadfast and true, this passing night confirms yet again that our enemies walk among us, that they hide behind masks.
>
> ...

> Beware of conspirators and traitors, and expose
> malicious rumormongers.
> ...
> Forward march, countrymen ... forward march ...
> forward march. (148)

This ultimately suggests that the regime is still closed off; it shuns communication and is terrified of dialogue.

Thirty years ago, Wannous addressed the defeat of 1967 using new tools to criticize the political environment, just as is happening now in the Arab world. People are collectively resisting authoritarian thought and practices in interactive ways to advance their desire for freedom. Where Wannous used political theatre as a contemporary cultural means for change, many Arab youth now resort to social media networks to organize protests that lead to revolution, which in turn disrupts, topples, or pushes the regime to the edge of collapse, as we see happening in Syria. The connection here is dialogue. Creating a dialogue within the theatre is an implicit call to launch a dialogue in reality: as a playwright, Wannous was interested in action not only for his characters but also for the audience. Thus, *Soirée* is an expression of Wannous's desire for a theatrical revolution that parallels the political reality and interacts with it.

Translated by Meris Lutz

Notes

1. Mustafa Alloush, "Humoum al-Masrah wa al-Insan fi al-Maahad al-Aali lil Funun al-Masrahiyeh" [Theatrical and Humanitarian Concerns at the High Institute of Dramatic Arts], *Tishreen*, June 20, 2011, http://tishreen.info/__archives.asp?FileName=873120582201106200438021.
2. Ablah Al Rouini, *Haky al-Taair: Saadallah Wannous* (Cairo: Dar Mirit, 2005), 146.

3. Ibid., 151.
4. For more on Wannous and heritage, see Hassan Ali Al Mukhalaf, *Tawzif al-Turath fi al-Masrah: Dirasah Tatbiqiyeh fi Masrah Saadallah Wannous* [Using Heritage in Theatre: An Applied Study of the Theatre of Saadallah Wannous] (Damascus: Al Awaail, 2000).
5. Abdel Razzaq Eid, "al-Hurriyeh/al-Maarifeh/al-Sultah fi Masrah Wannous" [Freedom/Knowledge/Power in Wannous's Plays], in *Saadallah Wannous: al-Insan al-Muthaqqaf al-Mubdi* [Saadallah Wannous: The Creative Intellectual], ed. Abdel Rahman Munif and Faisal Darraj (Damascus: Dar Kanaan, 2000), 114.
6. Saadallah Wannous, "Bayanat li Masrah Arabi Jadid" [Manifestos for a New Arab Theatre], in *al-Aamal al-Kamilah* [The Complete Works] (Damascus: Al Ahali, 1996), 3:53.
7. Ibid., 24.
8. Ibid., 36.
9. Saadallah Wannous, *Halfat Samar min ajl 5 Hizeiran* [Soirée for the 5th of June] (Beirut: Dar Al Adab, 1978), 131. Subsequent references to the pages of this publication appear in parentheses in the text.
10. Saadallah Wannous, *al-Ightisab* [*Rape*], in *al-Aamal al-Kamilah* [The Complete Works of Saadallah Wannous] (Damascus: Al Ahali, 1996), 2:166.
11. Faten Ali Ammar, *Wannous fi al-Masrah al-Arabi al-Hadith* [Wannous in Modern Arab Theatre] (Kuwait: Dar Suaad Al Sabah, 1999), 61.
12. Saadallah Wannous, *Medusa Tahdaq fi al-Hayat* [Medusa Staring at Life] (Beirut: Dar Al Adab, 2004), 79.
13. Some scholars divide Wannous's career into three periods, while others divide it into two.
14. Mohammad Ismail Bassal, *Qira-at Simiyaieh fi Masrah Saadallah Wannous: Nasous al-Tisaayenat Namuthajan* [Semiotic Readings of Saadallah Wannous: Focusing on the 1990 Texts] (Damascus: Dar Al Ahali, 2000), 96.
15. Ibid., 96–7.
16. Ali Ammar, *Wannous fi al-Masrah al-Arabi al-Hadith*, 92–3.
17. Hassan Attiyeh, "Siraa al-That al-Tarikhiyeh wa al-Thiqafiyeh fi Aamal Wannous al-Oula" [Internal Struggles of History and Culture in Wannous's Early Works], in Munif and Darraj, *Saadallah Wannous*, 74.
18. See his interview with Abla Al Ruwaini in *Haka al-Taer: Wannous* [Wannous: The Bird Who Spoke] (Cairo: Maktabat Al Usra, 2005), 140–56.
19. Abdel Rahman Munif and Faisal Darraj, introduction, in Munif and Darraj, *Saadallah Wannous*, 13.
20. David Bohm and Lee Nichol, *On Dialogue* (London: Routledge, 2006), 6.

21. Mikhail Bakhtin, *Problems of Dostoevsky's Poetics*, trans. Caryl Emerson (Minneapolis: University of Minnesota Press, 1984), 293.
22. Ali Ammar, *Wannous fi al-Masrah al-Arabi al-Hadith*, 29.
23. Al Ruwaini, *Haka al-Taer*, 154.
24. Bakhtin, *Problems of Dostoevsky's Poetics*, 110.
25. Ismail Fahad Ismail, *al-Kilmeh al-Faal fi Masrah Wannous: Dirasseh* [Speech-Actions in the Theatre of Wannous] (Beirut: Dar Al Adab, 1981), 7–8.
26. Lisa Wedeen, *Ambiguities of Domination: Politics, Rhetoric, and Symbols in Contemporary Syria* (Chicago: University of Chicago Press, 1999).
27. Edward W. Said, *Representations of the Intellectual: The 1993 Reith Lectures* (London: Vintage, 1994), 9.
28. Mohammad Mahmoud Rahouma, *al-Nass al-Ghaeb: Dirassah fi Masrah Wannous* [The Missing Text: A Study of the Theatre of Wannous] (Cairo: Maktabat Al Shabab, 1991), 116.

8

Emerging Playwrights in Syria

Meisoun Ali

Yam Mashhadi, Fares Al Dhahabi, Wael Qaddour, and Adnan Awde are emerging playwrights in Syria, and each developed a new play from 2008 to 2009 under the framework of the three major theatre initiatives of that period: the Damascus Arab Capital of Culture festival,[1] the Royal Court Theatre/British Council New Arab Playwrights Project,[2] and Tamasi.[3] These international cultural exchange programs provided institutional support that was and remains otherwise lacking for emerging talents. Given the dearth of government backing, these theatre artists, many of whom are graduates of the High Institute for Dramatic Arts in Damascus, have generally been left to fend for themselves and seek sponsorship from other sources. As the physical theatre artist Noura Murad[4] once told me, "I never want to work with the state institution; bureaucracy and art don't mix at all."

In autumn 2010, I conducted brief, individual interviews with the four aforementioned playwrights. These interviews, presented as the dialogue that follows, illuminate central concerns of contemporary playwrights in Syria.

> Yam Mashhadi: In light of the collapse of ideologies and failure of the socio-political project to implement change, we have turned to personal, internal topics that allow us to deal with the matters of everyday life.
>
> Fares Al Dhahabi: Indeed, today's generation of theatre artists chooses to present human stories and has abandoned the pursuit of ideological

causes. The prevailing conditions do not enable theatre to address what's going on.

Wael Qaddour: The reason is the retreat of politics in Syria.

YM: We are more concerned with our social freedom than we are with our political freedom.

WQ: Emerging writers put forth big ideas without citing facts that would cross the red line. When I write, I draw from within myself, I'm talking about my personal experience.

Adnan Awde: I don't want to burden my writing with direct political discourse. What I want to say is: Come, let's accept each other and make peace in order to know how to proceed.

FD: My questions are those of any young person who lives in Syria: Who am I? Am I an individual? How? What I say in my play *Molana* is that people can rebel with extreme simplicity, for the walls that surround us are imaginary boundaries.

YM: In my play *Paris in the Dark*, women long for their homelands but are unable to go back. Their personal problems overlap with those of certain Syrian young people: concerns about the economy, dreams of emigration, and feelings of helplessness. I present characters whose souls have been torn apart in their countries and who are no longer able to work. In my opinion, young people perform their identities when they express ... the daily anxiety that they endure just to secure a piece of bread and to have a normal romantic relationship. This is identity, not a declaration of belonging to a national group or sect.

AA: I have simple questions: Why do I live here? Who am I in this place? And what problems plague my society? In my opinion, Syrian society has yet to make peace with itself. In my play *Kohl Pot*, the division between Nadia and her family reflects the current division among Syrians.

YM: The search for identity requires a margin of freedom. The generation of the sixties and seventies had some sort of margin to work within while we work as individuals.

> WQ: I take on the problems in which I myself become entangled and drown. One of these issues is sex. Sex is surrounded by huge walls of silence and fear [even though] it is central to most of the tragic stories we hear in society, whether they are [stories of] repression or honor crimes. In my play *Virus*, I discuss sex, the beauty of relationships, and society's regressive attitude towards these issues – society's hypocrisy and contradictions.
>
> AA: My work carries intellectual inquiries about how I relate to the Other, [about how I relate] to institutions, beginning with the family and ending with the state.

The plays by Mashhadi, Al Dhahabi, Qaddour, and Awde reflect how the writers[5] focus on social, romantic, and sexual questions. Mashhadi's *Paris in the Dark* focuses on the experience of three women from Russia, Lebanon, and Syria, who share the experiences of emigration and exile, leaving behind homelands that cannot handle their spirits. Al Dhahabi's *Molana*, set in a poor Damascus neighborhood, is about rebellion against traditional religious mores: the protagonist, Abed, embraces his unique interpretation of Sufism and is consequently ostracized by society.

Qaddour's *Virus* also reveals how young men and women go against the grain by entering into romantic and sexual relationships before marriage. The text conveys characters not prepared to take responsibility for their relationships and decisions. For instance, a young man leaves the country, abandoning his pregnant girlfriend, who flees and hides from her family until she gives birth and sells her child. Another character deliberates the possibility of undergoing hymen reconstructive surgery and ultimately decides against it. Although other artistic and literary genres had addressed this issue, *Virus* may be the first play to broach the subject in Syrian theatre. Finally, *Kohl Pot* by Awde traces 80 years of Syrian history, beginning with the massacre of Armenians at Mount Ararat in 1917 and ending in the neighborhood of Muhajireen at the foot of Mount Qasyoun in Damascus. In the play, Gregor, an Armenian child, loses his family in the massacre and is found by a Bedouin and his wife who adopt him. Gregor is raised as an Arab Bedouin, growing up to marry a Circassian.

Whereas writers like Mustafa Al Hallaj (b. 1927), Walid Ikhlassi (b. 1935), Farhan Bulbul (b. 1935), Saadallah Wannous (1941–1997), and Mamdouh Udwan (1941–2004) adopted political, ideological, and nationalistic ideas as the pillars of their plays, today's generation has turned inward, focusing on the Self and addressing issues usually dealt with privately. The questions that preoccupied the older generation of playwrights in the 1960s included the following: what is theatre of a distinctly Arab and local identity? How can we achieve authenticity in both form and content? These questions emerged with the Pan-Arabism movements that swept the region nearly 50 years ago. At that time, Syrian theatre was at its peak; it enjoyed state support and relative creative independence.

The new generation is not interested in the lines of inquiry of the previous generation. Examining the texts of these playwrights, we see that what distinguishes them from the work of their predecessors is their handling of taboo subjects. Still, young writers' work tends to avoid more troubling or embarrassing questions, bearing in mind the standards of the censors. Young people generally tackle the themes of their plays descriptively without analyzing the political, social, and cultural context. The plays rely on the reader and audience to draw their own conclusions about context. The problem does not appear to be one of censorship so much as one of maturity and experience.

Based on a translation by Meris Lutz

Notes

1. In 2008, Damascus was the UNESCO Arab Capital of Culture and hosted hundreds of Arab and international cultural events. The Damascus Arab Capital

of Culture (DACC) and Dar Mamdouh Udwan collaborated to institute a new playwriting program. For a brief overview of how DACC affected cultural production, see Shayna Silverstein, "Local Meets Global at World Music Nights in Damascus," *Syrian Studies Association Newsletter*, 14, no. 1 (2008), https://ojcs.siue.edu/ojs/index.php/ssa/article/view/16/44.

2. For a summary of the program, which took place from April 2007 until February 2009, see British Council, "Dance: Call for Applications," accessed December 29, 2011, www.britishcouncil.org/morocco-arts-new-writing.htm.
3. A collaboration between the Swedish International Development Cooperation Agency and the Dramatiska Institutet, Tamasi is a civil society and performing arts initiative which aims to strengthen freedom of expression. In Syria, theatre scholar, professor, and translator Marie Elias has overseen Tamasi projects. See Stockholm's Academy of Dramatic Arts, "Sida Project – Tamasi," accessed December 29, 2011, www.stdh.se/in-english/international-projects/sida-project-tamasi.
4. For more on Noura Murad, see Khalil Sweileh, "Noura Murad: Dancing to Heal the Broken Arab Body," *Al Akhbar English*, September 3, 2011, http://english.al-akhbar.com/content/noura-murad-dancing-heal-broken-arab-body.
5. For more examples of contemporary playwriting from Syria, see *Hikaya al-Rouh wa al-Ismant: Arbaat Nusous Masrahiyyeh* [The Story of Soul and Cement: Four Plays], with an introduction by David Greig (Beirut: Dar Al Farabi, 2010). Published with the support of Culture Resource (Al Mawred Al Thaqafy), the collection includes *Bronze* by Mudhar Al Hajji, *Suad Braids Her Hair* by Soumar Daghastani, *Out of Control* by Wael Qaddour, and *Damascus-Aleppo* by Abdullah Al Kafri.

1 High Institute of Dramatic Arts, Damascus, Syria.

2 University lecture in Saadallah Wannous Theatre, High Institute of Dramatic Arts, Damascus, Syria.

3 Students and theatre professor Rania Jawad, Birzeit University, Occupied Palestinian Territories.

4 The Egyptian National Theatre in Ataba Square, Cairo, Egypt was gutted by a fire in 2008 and is still under renovation four years later.

5 Dalia Basiouny, playwright and performer, in Rawabet Theatre, Cairo, Egypt.

6 Rawabet Theatre, Cairo, Egypt.

7 Mohammad Attar, playwright, in Beirut, Lebanon.

8 Oussama Ghanem, theatre director,
in Al Qabbani Theatre, Damascus, Syria.

9 Abdullah Al Kafri, playwright, in Monnot Theatre, Beirut, Lebanon.

10 In 2011, Zeina Daccache, director and drama therapist, led a ten-month theatre project in Baabda Women's Prison in Lebanon, which culminated with the performance *Scheherazade in Baabda* in spring 2012.

11 Collectif Kahraba, a theatre collective, in Mar Mikhaël Annahr, Beirut, Lebanon.

12 Founded in 1965, Beirut Theatre in Lebanon was forced to close its doors in December 2011. A recent ministerial decree declared the building a national heritage structure to stave off demolition, but in light of the frequent inefficacy of such decrees, its fate remains unknown.

13 Fadi Abi Samra, actor, and Issam Boukhaled, director, in Beirut Theatre, Lebanon.

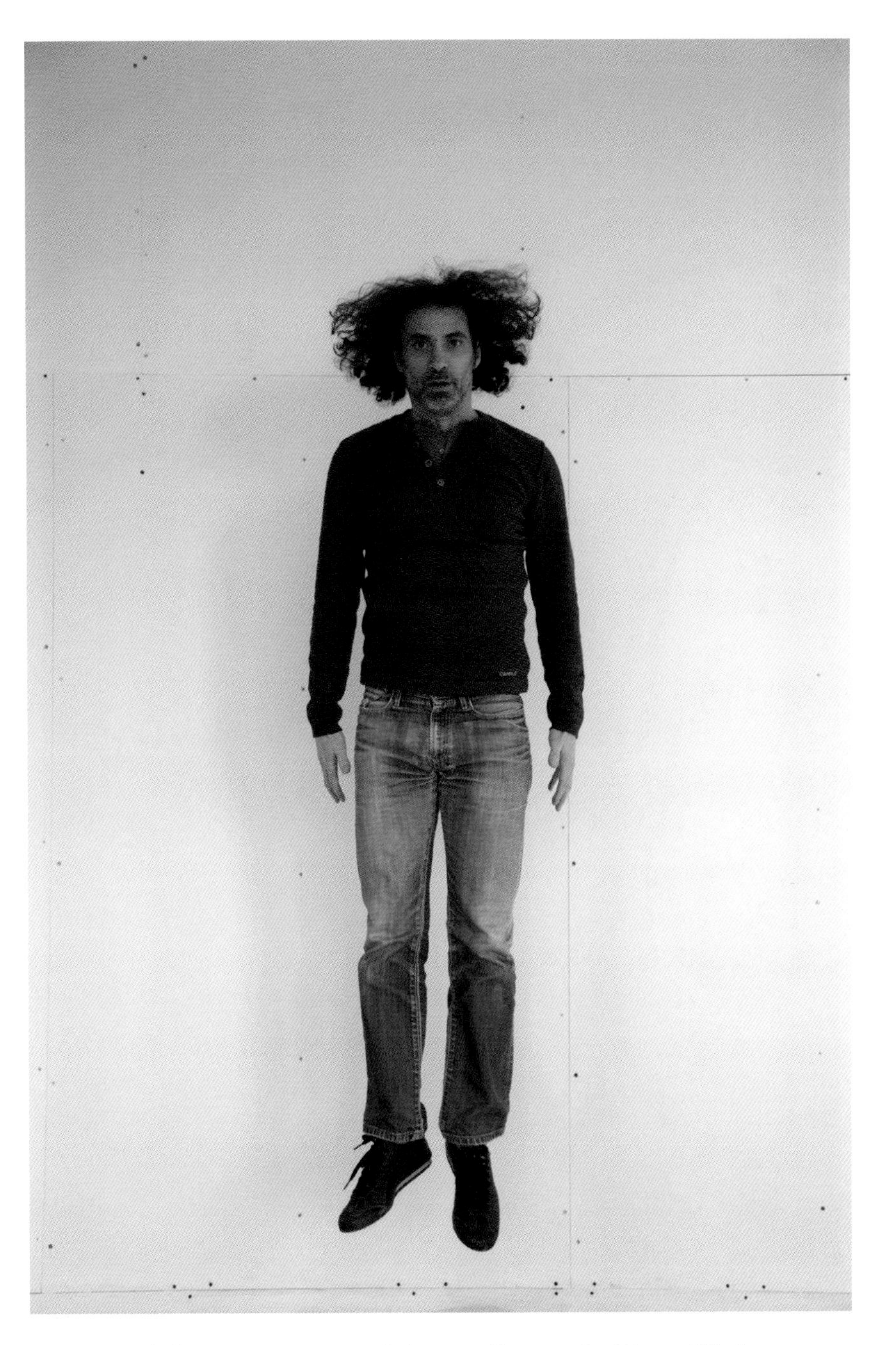

14 Rabih Mroué, actor and theatre director, in Home Workspace, Beirut, Lebanon.

15 Sulayman Al Bassam, writer and theatre director, in the Bristol Hotel, Beirut, Lebanon.

16 Jennifer Jajeh, actor and writer, in her residence, San Francisco, California.

17 Jawad Al Asadi, playwright and director, in Babel Theatre, Beirut, Lebanon.

9

Practicing Theatre and Playwriting in Damascus

Abdullah Al Kafri

A quick glance at theatre infrastructure in Syria, and the challenges immediately come to light. There are only five timid performance halls in the capital attempting to serve more than 5 million citizens in metropolitan Damascus. In addition to the infrastructure deficit, bureaucratic procedures are tedious and time-consuming, and institutional support is wanting. Practicing theatre has become an exercise in waiting in line for permits, licenses, and approvals. In the past decade, theatrical activity has all but vanished from the halls of the establishment, namely the Directorate of Theatre and Music[1] and the National Theatre, leaving devoted independent practitioners with little or no recourse to make theatre. The profession itself, which used to be unfettered by bureaucracy, has become reliant on independent administration in the absence of official institutional support.

Performances occur rarely and are indistinguishable from one another, contributing to a mechanical monotony. The number of shows produced in Syrian cities other than Damascus amounts to less than a handful per year. For instance, Daraa, Hasaka, and Idlib may see one performance every two years; most theatre initiatives there are doomed to remain in the project development phase without ever coming to fruition. Today's generation of theatre practitioners, including those in Damascus, have dreamt of theatre more than they have seen it: they have read more than they have attended, discussed more than they have participated, and imagined more than they have embodied.

They are tired of unoriginal, amateur works, tired of theatre productions by people who are disconnected from reality. For more than 50 years, the National Theatre has been the primary body of theatre production, and independent troupes have long had to seek the Directorate of Theatre and Music's approval for both texts and performances. Perhaps practitioners in today's generation have given up on their desire for representation by a single entity, one which thinks on their behalf and takes the reigns of creativity out of their hands. The disconnect between these national organizations and theatre makers of today has led practitioners to find alternative solutions.

This generation counts among its ranks writers, directors, set designers, and critics who are stymied in their work due to the lack of infrastructure, the difficulty of executing their projects, and the scarcity of platforms for constructive theatre criticism. There are no administrative frameworks like those which enabled the theatre practitioners of the 1970s and 1980s, such as Saadallah Wannous, Fawaz Al Sajir, Nayla Al Atrash, and Walid Qawtali, to present full-fledged theatrical productions. Since the mid 1990s, large-scale projects have dwindled, giving way to individual and scattered performances and experimental theatre initiatives. The dire need for independent cultural administration and for the funding of independent projects has, consequently, led to a growing interest in arts management. In the past five years, particularly since the year-long Damascus Arab Capital of Culture festival in 2008, regional organizations such as Al Mawred Al Thaqafy (Culture Resource) and local institutions like the High Institute of Dramatic Arts have promoted opportunities to develop arts administration skills though new course offerings, workshops, and seminars.

* * *

Today's generation of multidisciplinary theatre makers, who trained in European and Syrian humanities programs as well as in architecture and design departments,[2] seeks greater integration into international theatre movements and a more dynamic relationship with the audience. Since the 1950s, translation of international theatrical texts into Arabic has dwindled. Theatre practitioners seek to reverse this trend and, in so doing, engage more substantially with global theatre culture. This interest in the international sphere stands alongside a commitment to reflecting on the nation and society, particularly in the wake of critical political, economic, and social changes and subsequent artistic developments. In light of the changes of the past decade, theatre makers are asking: how do audiences relate to theatre? How should they relate to theatre? Why are we making this type of theatre, here and now, and who is our audience?

In that regard, an autumn 2008 production of *The Emigrés* (1975) by Polish playwright Slawomir Mrozek signaled a shift in the relationship between the theatrical text and the audience.[3] The play features two immigrants, an intellectual and a worker, who share a basement apartment and struggle with the anguish of exile and diaspora. Adapted and directed by Samer Omran with dramaturgy by Oussama Ghanem, the play was performed by Omran and Mohamad Al Rashee and presented in a public bomb shelter adjacent to a cemetery in Damascus.

Diverse audiences, old and young, thronged to *The Emigrés*, which ran for months and was later produced in the United Arab Emirates as part of the Sharjah Biennial in 2009. The performance style was simple and minimalist, and audiences crammed tightly into the shelter, resulting in a startlingly intimate theatrical experience. The audience was literally present on the stage, nearly within arm's reach of the actors. *The Emigrés* exemplified a movement towards realism in Syrian theatre today, towards simple and succinct dialogue and the adoption and reinterpretation of foreign texts in the context of contemporary Syrian society. Other examples of successful adaptation of foreign texts include *An Enemy of the People* (1882) by Henrik Ibsen, produced in 2008 with Mohamad Al Attar as dramaturg, and *The Zoo Story* (1958) by Edward Albee, produced in 2010.[4]

* * *

The end of the last decade in Syria, and in Damascus in particular, witnessed a surge in playwriting. Unfortunately, many of the plays that have emerged in recent years have not been published. Those who turned to playwriting were generally in their mid-thirties or younger, and the trend was accompanied by a spate of programs and educational opportunities.[5]

For instance, in 2007 the British Council in Damascus launched a collaboration with the Royal Court Theatre and playwright David Greig. The program aimed to implement a multiyear playwriting workshop that culminated in the publication of new plays and the presentation of staged readings, collectively framed under the title "We Come From Here." Performances were based throughout the Arab world, as well as in London and New York City. The French Cultural Center in Damascus has also organized staged readings for French and Syrian playwrights. Honor killings, urban life, the role of religion in society, generational differences, and social isolation were central themes in new plays such as *Kohl Pot* (2009) by Adnan Awde, *Virus* (2008) by Wael Qaddour, and *Bronze* (2011) and *Five Days in the Eyes of the Devil* (2008) by Mudhar Al Hajji.

The playwrights share a desire to experiment with playwriting as a tool for examining the structure of society. They aim to read society, envisage it in fine detail, and reveal its dark corners. They have come to abandon the ideological currents that characterized dramatic texts of their predecessors, yet their work shares the depth and spirit of plays by people like of Wannous and the late Mamdouh Udwan. These new playwrights wrestle with the role and influence of television dialogue on speech in theatre just as they grapple with the differences between Modern Standard Arabic versus colloquial speech and dialects. There is a tendency to deploy colloquial dialects instead of conventional Standard Arabic as a vehicle of contemporary intellectual discourse.

Despite the flurry of playwriting, emerging writers face a number of obstacles in their efforts to stage new plays. Firstly, due to limited financial resources, most directors choose texts that require few actors and inexpensive set design and production. Secondly, most Syrian directors, whether in film or theatre, prefer foreign texts rather than local texts, despite their relevance to the local context. They deem the work of emerging Syrian playwrights to lack artistic maturity. Thirdly, audiences tend to judge new experiments in dramatic writing based on how accurately they reflect reality. Audience responses to new playwriting often revolve, almost exclusively, around how probable or realistic a particular scenario may be.

* * *

Artists seeking to stage new and experimental theatre have thus sought financial support primarily from international sources but also from a few local foundations. For example, the Zurich-based Drosos Foundation funded a two-year project, “Interactive Theatre in Public Schools,” under the purview of Rawafed, the cultural arm of the Syria Trust for Culture and Development. The Swedish International Development Cooperation Agency partnered with Dar Al Assad (the Damascus Opera House) to fund five theatre performances by young people, including *Kohl Pot*, directed by Omar Abu Saada in 2009. The General Authority of Dar Al Assad itself has begun offering direct financial support to certain productions.

A few of the more daring contemporary theatre productions have also received support from these and other donors, such as the Arab Fund for Arts Culture, Al Mawred Al Thaqafy, and the Hivos Fund based in the

Netherlands. *It Happened Tomorrow*, directed by Oussama Ghanem in 2010, broached taboo subjects of sexual, social, and religious freedom. These productions, which have widened the horizons of discourse in the theatre, have revealed that the ceiling of censorship needs to be repaired and that the empty space below it filled before it can be lifted.

* * *

More collaboration between the state institutions – the National Theatre and the Directorate – and the new generation of dramatists could resolve many of these challenges. Should the national institutions wish to revive Syrian theatre, administrators ought to realize the necessity of redrawing the relationship with independent theatre initiatives and deepening the engagement with those artists.

Based on a translation by Meris Lutz

Notes

1. The Directorate of Theatre and Music was established in Syria in 1958 and currently falls under the umbrella of the Ministry of Culture.
2. The High Institute of Dramatic Arts in Damascus established a set design department in 2002.
3. See Meris Lutz, "Play Underground," *The National* (Abu Dhabi), June 9, 2009, www.thenational.ae/arts-culture/art/play-underground.
4. For more on this performance of *The Zoo Story*, see Ali Wajjih, "Aan 'Qussit Hadiqat Al Hayawan' Allati Atharet Jadallan Wassaan Lede al-Jamhour al-Sourie" [On *The Zoo Story*, the Play that Stirred Up Controversy among Syrian Audiences], *Bostah*, July 10, 2010, www.bostah.com/news/reportages/10629--1-r-.
5. This section of the essay was presented as a working paper titled "Language in Search of its Audience" at the 15th edition of the Damascus Theatre Festival, Damascus, December 29, 2010. The entire essay was authored in spring 2011.

10

12 Angry Lebanese in Roumieh Prison

Zeina Daccache

Bored. I was bored of theatre in Beirut, theatre in Lebanon. Bored of the vicious and incestuous cycle of theatre: your colleagues attend your shows, you go to their shows, together we go to another artist's shows. This is how I felt after university, in the first years of my "professional life."

Where was the audience? Isn't theatre supposed to be for an audience? Or have we isolated ourselves as theatre artists by obsessing over the mere act of creation, while losing sight of society and a greater civilizational hunger? But what do we even mean by audience, by society? The people we see on the way to work in the morning? The baker? The taxi driver? Our colleagues?

Are these people in our offices? The university? What about those people in places we may not think about or visit regularly? The Beirut streets inhabited by immigrants, the rehabilitation centers that welcome those suffering from drug addiction, or what about the mentally ill patients in forgotten hospitals, or the 7,000 inmates crammed into prisons throughout the country?

So, I started to wonder: if the messages conveyed by the "artists" are boring and if that is why the audiences are always the same, maybe the artists should come from the other half – the much larger portion of society – people with something in their gut, something concrete to say. I wanted to test a hypothesis: theatre can live in the most forgotten places and grow in the most difficult situations.

My pursuit of this hypothesis led me to London in 2000, where I studied with Philippe Gaulier, who always used to say, "If you're boring as an actor, try banking." For Philippe, theatre was an emancipatory tool for anyone and everyone – his workshops included lawyers, accountants, and librarians who would take a sabbatical year to practice theatre. Two years later, I saw this same philosophy at work in Volterra Prison in Italy, where I had a stint assisting Italian theatre director Armando Punzo in the prison.

Around that time, I began working at Oum El Nour, a rehabilitation center for recovering addicts in Lebanon. I didn't know it yet, but I had already begun practicing drama therapy. I headed to the United States, to Kansas State University in 2006 to begin my drama therapy graduate studies, based on the premise that theatre plays a therapeutic role in our lives.

When I returned to Lebanon, I founded the nonprofit organization Catharsis, with the objective of bringing theatre and drama therapy to society ... the real one. My first impulse was to work with people living behind the walls of Lebanese prisons. My experience in Volterra Prison had inspired me to do something similar in my own country. So, I applied for a European Union grant to implement a drama therapy project in the largest detention center for men in Lebanon: Roumieh Prison.

My objectives, as I wrote before setting foot inside the prison, were to rehabilitate a room/venue as a theatre inside Roumieh Prison, to facilitate drama therapy sessions for around 40 prisoners, and to produce a play inside the prison. By staging the performance inside the penitentiary, the project sought to open the prison to a wide external audience, forming a bridge between the inmates and the outside world. Soon enough the project evolved, and we pursued even greater ambitions: the play became part of an awareness campaign to abolish the death penalty, to implement laws for the reduction of sentences based on good behavior records, to respect the equality of prisoners before the law, and to promote their judicial and social rights.

My colleagues and I at Catharsis wanted to change the ways in which the public perceived prisoners, to foster a view of prisoners as real people combating stereotypes and misperceptions that label them sinners, criminals, or losers. We wanted to demonstrate how vibrant and illuminating a prisoner's perspective could be.

After the EU green-lighted the project in 2007, we faced the challenge of explaining the project to Lebanese government officials, who thought I was crazy to believe that theatre – a luxury, in their opinion – was a must for the prison. They refused again and again, but I was stubborn and kept insisting. They finally approved our request to start the project but required that we ask for all kinds of approvals at each step of the way.

We were granted a permit to work in a room in Block D, the building that houses inmates awaiting their sentences, some of whom have been waiting several years. I loved the room. It was huge, kind of a hangar, walls rotten from the rain, and a wall of windows made the light inside the room amazing. Until that point, the room was used mainly for religious purposes such as Friday prayer and Sunday mass.

It was an oxygen reservoir in the prison. It was the "safe space" that we look for as drama therapists, the best theatre venue the site had to offer. I didn't want to change a thing in the room, aside from adding some seating, curtains, and minimal electrical equipment.

Two hundred and fifty inmates responded to the call for auditions. Few had ever done theatre, but they were excited about it and the chance to be heard – they knew audiences would attend. Others were reluctant and doubtful of the project. To them, we seemed like just another group of people coming to sell hope but never achieving what we set out to do.

All I could say was that time would tell. Their attitude, coupled with the endless bureaucratic hurdles and the difficulty of working in a prison, led me to wonder if I'd really be able to persevere and see the project through.

Of the 250 inmates, 45 were selected to participate in the theatre production, with priority going to those facing the death penalty or a life sentence. We also favored inmates who showed motivation during the two-month workshop conducted at the beginning of the process to identify and welcome potential participants. We needed about 15 months of rehearsal, and as an actress, I knew that such a commitment would not be easy.

The process began, and it was a journey of challenging and unforgettable moments. At one point I cast Youssef, who had served 18 years of a life sentence, but the authorities refused because of his bad behavior record. He was shouting and crying, "That's unjust!" I saw how eager he was and how beautifully he engaged in the exercises during the preliminary workshop, so I approached the administration. As it turned out, they had crossed their wires: their files were inaccurate. The record besmirched with bad behavior was not Youssef's, but belonged to someone else. I will never forget Youssef's smile when he was finally accepted.

Hawillo, a 63-year-old inmate who was serving five years for drug dealing, panicked when he heard he was cast in a leading role. "But I can't read," he said. So, we secured a permit to get him an MP3 player and had his friends record his lines, about 20 pages, all of which he memorized at night, even though he didn't entirely understand them all.

I decided to stage an adaptation of *Twelve Angry Men*, a 1954 play by American writer Reginald Rose. The play follows a jury deliberating the death sentence for an 18-year-old accused of killing his father. Eleven members of the jury are wholly convinced that the suspect is guilty and refuse to reconsider the case, guided by deep prejudice and faulty judgments that nearly lead them to a miscarriage of justice. In our Roumieh adaptation, titled *12 Angry Lebanese*, the members of the jury were played by inmates, resulting in a reversal of roles. The inmates played our role, the presumably objective society judging and debating the fate of a suspect on trial.

Roumieh represents a microcosm of Lebanon and the sectarian groups that form the national polity. Thus, our adaptation also occasioned interaction and dialogue between these divergent socio-political constituencies. As the jury argues about the defendant's case, they get sidetracked by their own agendas, ignorance, and stereotyping. In that regard, the production conveyed the situation not only of prisoners but also of socio-politics in Lebanon.

Each actor – each inmate – brought his unique life experience to the adaptation. The performance was punctuated by monologues, personal testimonies that we carefully developed during the rehearsal period. Topics included the struggle of the inmates with the death penalty law and with the years, or decades, of incarceration. We also enlisted some of the musically inclined inmates to create a soundtrack for the play; they ended up performing twelve songs during each performance.

Every day, the actors brought in monologues, texts, and songs they wanted to integrate into the performance. Most of them were stories or suggestions for new laws. This process led us to create a group for monologues, and each member of the group would perform a monologue in the play.

Rateb, sentenced to seven years for rape, proposed a monologue repenting his crime. Some of the other men threatened to leave the group if Rateb performed the piece. "We can't work with a criminal," they said. I couldn't believe it. Wow. I replied: "If that's the case, then I'm heading out because I can't work with 45 criminals! Either you shut up, or you all quit and leave Rateb to work alone."

After 15 months of preparation, the play saw the light of day in February 2009. We staged eight shows over a two-month period at Roumieh Prison. Every performance brought about 300 audience members, including officials, ministers, deputies, ambassadors, journalists, and human rights activists. The final show, on Mother's Day, was exclusively for the inmates' families. The actors spent three hours with family members, a record in Roumieh history.

One February afternoon following the first two performances, during a meeting with the group in prison to discuss our progress and to iron out some kinks in the performance, the men informed me that one of the actors, Hussein, a musician and a dancer in the play, was unexpectedly released that morning. We still had six more performances to go. I was happy for him but felt exhausted by working in moving sands. One day, I got a permit; the next day, it was rejected. One day, an inmate was singing and dancing; the next day, he was gone.

I was leaving the prison, mulling over this emotional rollercoaster, and to my surprise I saw Hussein waiting at the gate on the day of his release, saying, "Let me in now! No way, I'm not going to drop what I've built for the first time in my life. I need to come back – please get me a permit to enter with you." We got a permit for Hussein to enter the prison as a "civilian" and to perform in the six remaining performances. If there was ever any doubt, now everyone was sure we were both crazy.

12 Angry Lebanese wrapped up in April 2009, and one month later, the Ministry of Justice in collaboration with the Ministry of the Interior implemented the early release law 463/2002 – the law of sentence reduction, issued in 2002 but never implemented. We had advocated consistently for this law through *12 Angry Lebanese.*

We continued our drama therapy sessions, but this time with around 200 inmates and with funding from the Italian Embassy. Most of the *Angry* actors attended, and many assisted us in including and working closely with new participants.

Hawillo, the illiterate actor whom we all loved for his sense of humor, was diagnosed with cancer in 2010. We were devastated. He was relocated to a hospital, where I visited him every day. Due to his failing health, I sought an amnesty for him so that he could spend his final months at home with his family and not in the prison hospital. He died in the hospital three months later, the same day that he was granted amnesty. We faced a void. It was a rough time, especially for the inmates with life sentences. "Sooner or later, we'll all follow Hawillo," they would say. What could I say or do?

Six months later, Majdi also died of cancer. He was a 60-year-old Egyptian with no family in Lebanon, and so I had to call his family in Egypt to inform them of his passing.

At that point, I was crushed. I hit rock bottom. I had to accept that the web of bureaucracy and permits made everything impossible in Lebanon. Despite my hopelessness, I had to persevere and continue working with the men, even though I wasn't convinced by what I was doing anymore. Was theatre really the solution? Was I fooling myself and the group? All I could think about was that if Majdi or Hawillo had been imprisoned in a different country, if they hadn't had to deal with the stifling Lebanese bureaucracy, they might have escaped death. Youssef, whose record was mismatched when we began the project but participated in the play after we clarified the matter with the prison administration, started to ask the most challenging questions. "Zeina, why are we doing theatre? Do you think it will change our destiny to die in this place?"

After two years of essentially living in the prison, I wasn't even sure what role I should play, or who I should be in this difficult situation. The theatre person? The psychologist? The impromptu lawyer? The human rights advocate? Doctor? Activist? Or was I all of these?

I'd say to Youssef, "You answer: tell me. Why?" He'd tell me that theatre might change things. It gave him hope that the limits of prison walls are never impossible to overcome. When I had hit rock bottom, it was the inmates who kept their faith in theatre.

In April 2011, a riot broke out in Roumieh Prison, and Block D erupted into flames. The entire ground floor was burned, including the theatre room, just two months before the opening of our second theatre production. I couldn't believe it.

When I went to visit the site, I was speechless, certain that we had to close up shop. But one of the actors said to me, "Zeina, if I can face my life sentence, you've got to face this challenge. Let's reconstruct the theatre." Sure enough, Catharsis, the nonprofit organization that administers the drama therapy project, expects funding from the High Relief Council to do just that. But who knows when it will come through?

Challenges, limits, hurdles, again and again. This time, it was too much. I have realized that this is a place where sometimes you have to acknowledge that things are beyond your control. And coming to terms with that is very difficult.

If we give up, if I stop, what will I do? It is clear as day. I could never fall back on boredom, not me. If Youssef and others are sentenced to life in prison, then I guess I am sentenced to a life of believing that theatre has and will always go beyond the limits of reality.

11

What has Slipped Away is So Far, and What is Yet to Come So Close

Rabih Mroué

In his play *Rape* (1990), Saadallah Wannous "breaks the laws" of his country. Syrian law forbids citizens from meeting or speaking with Israelis, regardless of their political inclinations or of the location of the meeting, under penalty of prosecution for charges ranging from cultural normalization and dealing with the enemy to treason. Despite these risks, Wannous decided to speak with Dr. Abraham Menuhin, a Jewish resident of Israel. The two exchanged ideas and held discussions before Dr. Menuhin was arrested by Israeli security and committed to a psychiatric institution. The conversation between them took place in the doctor's clinic in Israel, and it is registered in a small book issued by the Dar Al Adab publishing house in Lebanon in 1990. This conversation spans four pages and contains 36 questions and answers. The responses are divided equally between the two men, and the discussion ends with empathy and an invitation to exchange 'pity and perhaps even hope' for their predicament.[1]

As far as I know, not one law-abiding citizen of Syria or Lebanon (where the book was published) has initiated a lawsuit against Wannous. No one has accused him of contact with the enemy following his 'probable dialogue' with a Jewish doctor, which took place in the latter's clinic in Israel. No arrest warrant was issued against him, nor did the security apparatuses of either state move to follow or detain him for investigation. In my opinion, this is due not to the Syrian regime's complacency or tolerance of Wannous or to a national, political, intellectual consciousness that grasps the importance of this 'probable dialogue.' Nor is it due to the security forces' ignorance of the meeting. Rather, Wannous was left alone because the meeting and dialogue took place in an ambiguous space where the law is powerless, or at the very least confused: the world of art, and specifically the world of theatre, is a space of fiction where there are presumably no real-world consequences for a person's actions. For this reason, the conversation between the Syrian Wannous and the Jewish/Israeli doctor remains where it began – in the world of art, of fiction, not reality, even though such a meeting could actually occur.

Whereas the words "hypothetical" or "theoretical" connote fantasy, unreality, and impossibility, "probable" describes that which is possible and realizable. Here lies the importance of the remarkable stage direction at the end of the play, where Wannous indicates that his interview with the doctor is a 'probable dialogue.' Wannous could have written a hypothetical or imagined dialogue but insisted on using the word "probable" because the probable is possible. Here lies the danger and risk of this dialogue, wherein Wannous admits, in the presence of the Israeli doctor, to having had to overcome many obstacles to meet with him.

Among these obstacles is the 'historical suspicion that prevents recognition of the existence' of the doctor and those like him – Jewish Israelis opposed to Zionism – as well as the 'political demagogy which prevents differentiating' between other Israelis and those like the doctor, 'the vanquished's fear of deception, the isthmus of victims and wounds, the checkpoints and ploys of the police and the spy hunters,' and the barriers erected inside and around Wannous himself. These many obstacles – psychological, security-related, historical, and political – required great courage on the part of Wannous.

The fact that this meeting between these two men even took place opens a new realm of possibilities.

By simply presenting itself on stage as a probable yet unrealized action, the conversation becomes an ambiguous act caught between fiction and reality. This is the terrain that confuses authority, censors, and even the audience, complicating the applicability of the law. If the probable dialogue left the realm of art or theatre and entered that of politics or the media, the probable act would approach reality, narrowing the limits of ambiguity and confusion and allowing the law to operate more clearly. This would have had grave consequences for Wannous who could have been thrown in prison or forced to seek asylum in exile.

This is what happened, for example, to the Lebanese writer and poet Bilal Khbeiz, who published a newspaper article in 2008 in the cultural supplement of *Annahar*, where he worked as deputy editor. In this article, he described the city of Tel Aviv without having visited it in an attempt to break the same barriers faced by Wannous. Because of this article, a group of so-called law-abiding citizens accused him of normalization with the Zionist enemy, prompting the owner of *Annahar*, Ghassan Tueni, to stop publishing Khbeiz's writing. He was then threatened with death by unknown parties and became the subject of various rumors, including that he worked as a regular correspondent for the Israeli newspaper *Haaretz* and that he was collaborating with the Israeli enemy by serving the Mossad. These eventually forced Khbeiz into exile. He became a victim of injustice because he did not think that his imagined visit to an Israeli city, which he decided to perform in the realm of journalism and which he chronicled without setting foot there, would end in disaster: threats on his life and being forced to leave the country.

I suppose that if Khbeiz's article had appeared in the art world, maybe none of that would have happened. One cannot play in the world of politics and media as one is allowed to play in the world of art and theatre. It is common knowledge that censorship in the Arab world prevents "playing" or "law-breaking" under any pretext, whether it be theatre, journalism, or otherwise. But this is what makes Wannous's meeting all the more important, especially if this game, this bending of the law, comes as a critique of the system and authorities. The reasons for the significance of the meeting are plain, and I will discuss some of them in this essay.

The institutions of art – theatre, film, video, and conceptual art, for instance – are among the rare spaces where one *may* be permitted to depart from the law and social norms. I emphasize may because permission in these spaces is conditional upon social, political, psychological, economic, and legislative circumstances which widen or narrow the realm of possibility. To some extent, that permission remains broad and guaranteed under the laws of democratic states that respect their own legal systems and protect the freedom of their citizens. However, permission remains narrow and practically unobtainable in security states or totalitarian states, such as the one in which Saadallah Wannous lived.

In modern democratic states, one can, through the world of art and its institutions, step outside the law for a few hours before going back to being a loyal citizen. Here lies the importance of theatre as a place of agitation and dissent. In the name of theatre, an actor or artist can commit acts that he or she cannot commit outside the theatre. He or she can talk about taboos and open debates on serious issues such as religion, sex, armies, war, treason, and so on – publicly, before an audience. The artist can also, within his or her art, inflict physical harm on his or her body without it being considered a breach of law. Examples are numerous and sundry: Chris Burden was shot in the hand with a rifle as part of his work *Shoot*; Marina Abramovic took excessive amounts of medication to the point where it nearly killed her, all before a live audience, in her performance *Rhythm 2*; Gina Pane cut herself with razors. All of these acts would have moved courts to legal prosecution if they were committed outside the institution of art. The institution of art in those countries protects its artists' freedom to a large degree.

I posit that the theatre is a space of probability, a space in which one can play with the law, a space to break taboos and destabilize rigid beliefs in order to hold accountable ourselves and others, a space for breaking deadly binaries and doubting what we take for granted, distancing ourselves from postulates and beliefs that hinder the movement of thought to the point of killing it. It is a space to raise issues, simple or complex, and to place them on the table of dialogue.

Wannous's probable meeting may be an exception to the rule in the Arab world, a rule which forbids any work of art that opposes authority. Wannous's extraordinary conversation is evidence of the urgent need for dialogue, and of the hunger for dialogue, both within ourselves and within the group to which we belong, before dialogue with the Other. What we need today is a completely open dialogue with no restrictions or conditions, dialogue aimed at provoking ourselves before provoking others, dialogue like the one described by Wannous in his message for the 1996 World Theatre Day, dialogue that is 'diverse, complex, and comprehensive – dialogue between individuals and dialogue between groups.'

But how can this kind of dialogue take place in countries ruled by rigid, despotic regimes and warring sects, in countries where laws and customs aim to paralyze institutions, trade unions, citizens, and their civil rights? How can such a dialogue begin in security states under emergency laws that strip citizens of their right to express their views, states that keep their citizens under surveillance by security agents and their thugs? How can dialogue begin in the complete absence of democracy and the rejection of pluralism and difference of opinion? How can theatre exist in a state with no institutions, where the law is either ignored or arbitrarily implemented to maintain the authority of the ruler and his entourage? How can theatre play an effective role when contemplation, reflection, and questioning assumptions and taboos are considered treason and heresy, a crime that must be punished?

The trial of Russian poet Joseph Brodsky, which took place in 1964 in the Soviet Union, raised questions about the meaning of work and production and the ways in which they are understood in totalitarian states. In totalitarian states, intellectual activity that does not fit the ideology of the regime is considered that of idle people who, as Adolf Hitler wrote in *Mein Kampf*, "impede the wheel of history." Therefore, those who engage in this type of work must be tried and punished for their failure to perform their national duty, which requires them to be part of the great state machine that works non-stop; there is no time for reflecting or thinking or writing. Everything must be in the service of the one and only rhetoric – that of the state.

Totalitarian authority robs its citizens of life by wearing them down with long hours of physically demanding work or trivial tasks, routines that exhaust the body and require no thought. There is no time left for thinking, formulating opinions, or debate. In the cycle of hard, routine, daily work, there is no time for the work of the mind. Here lies the importance of theatre and its role in allowing the audience to contemplate, to think and try and formulate ideas that restore our humanity. As Aristotle wrote, what separates human beings from animals is that people are capable of formulating abstract ideas. The question, then, has to do with the distribution of time between the elected members of the authority and the majority of people. Those who do not have time cannot formulate ideas. The issue, therefore, is not only the distribution of production and surplus production but of time as well. In the words of Jacques Rancière, he who has the time has the power.

The Arab world today is witnessing revolutions, changes, and geopolitical upheavals that must challenge axiomatic notions about the relationship of the citizen to power, the relationship between power and the state, the meaning of the modern state, the protection of citizens' civil rights, the safeguarding of individual freedom of thought and expression, and the role of political parties.

Today, the whole world is facing a difficult moral question regarding the citizen's right to maintain a margin of freedom, a space of intimacy under his or her sole jurisdiction, without being forced by anyone to disclose small secrets or to surrender personal space, which is protected by civil laws. In recent years, and particularly after the attacks of September 11, 2001, the major world powers mobilized and were followed by smaller countries in their fight against terrorism. Their main preoccupation became tracking down terrorists, but they went forth in this undertaking without ever establishing a clear definition of "terrorist" or specifying his or her location, thus placing their own citizens under the microscope of surveillance with the possibility of being monitored and suspected.

In the name of combating terrorism, these countries have sanctioned new provisions and passed laws that decree a kind of open-ended state of emergency, a more lenient version than that which we have experienced in some Arab countries. From the spread of surveillance cameras to the request that all citizens be fingerprinted, to magnetic identity cards by which security services can track an individual's movement, to wiretapping and more, citizens have found themselves forced to accept these new conditions and waive some of their civil rights in return for security and the ability to live in peace.

Since declaring the war on terror, the modern civil state has fallen in danger of becoming more like the security state, where all citizens are suspects until proven innocent. With the decline of the modern democratic state in favor of its security counterpart, how can theatre operate and preserve its distinctive features?

The security state assumes the right to put everyone under suspicion; it sanctions its own ability to arrest citizens and incarcerate them without issuing warrants, subpoenas, or other documents from relevant authorities. Suspicion is sufficient grounds for a citizen to be arrested and interrogated, for his or her personal history and professional or intimate relationships to be rifled through and examined. The citizen can be imprisoned without a trial, a defense lawyer, without even evidence or witnesses, and of course without the presence of the judge. An emergency court limits the justice system to carrying out the work of the police and security apparatuses. Resistance against states of emergency or wars is unacceptable and suspect since that would threaten the nation and undermine unity and security. When faced with danger or an enemy, there is no time for ideas or arguments, and there is certainly no place for "idle people."

If the civil state has been subsumed by the security state and the duties of its courts annulled, what does that mean for theatre?

Trials comprise elements which provide rich material for theatre practitioners: the stage and the audience, the opening session, one actor representing the public and another representing the accused, the representation of justice in the body of a judge, re-enacting the crime and its motives according to a narrative of facts, the plea, the appearance of the accused to face the witnesses before a panel of judges, the presence of police to control the uproar inside the chamber, even the unique garb of the court and the gavel strikes announcing the adjournment of the session.

Under the law, the trial is an event which brings together two opposing parties; each side presents its point of view using arguments and evidence before a panel of judges and a jury. The jurors listen and bear witness in the end to the ruling of the judge, who works in the name of the law and justice, independent from the legislative and executive branches. It is the right of the criminal, no matter how terrible or violent his or her crime, to appoint a brilliant lawyer to defend him before the judge. It is the duty of this lawyer to try his best to prove his client's innocence or win him or her a lighter sentence.

In theatre, as in the courtroom, different points of view are presented and attached to intense debates, arguments, and interrogations while the case and contextual factors are reviewed. In my opinion, the playwright, like the judge, must be neutral in drawing his or her characters in a simplistic and straightforward manner, without showing his or her bias towards a certain party over another. He or she gives each side and each person the time needed to prepare their case, evidence, and contextual factors necessary to present their views. But what distinguishes the stage from the court is that the former offers no final judgment in favor of either party. Theatre merely presents a subject from various perspectives, leaving space for members of the audience to build their own, perhaps differing, opinions on the proposed topic. Theatre is a place to postpone answers and judgment.

Theatre is the perfect place to raise and dive into complex, thorny issues. It is the place where ideas are formulated and where one can pose questions without reaching a final verdict. Theatre is not the mouthpiece of one particular side, whoever that may be, not even of the victim. Rather, the victim is the subject of discussion and reflection. The purpose of theatre is to search for and emphasize differences, and to hold discussions around them. The simplification of thorny issues into easy binaries, reducing characters to the victim and the executioner, hiding behind the claim of victimhood to defend or demand rights, is nothing but an attempt to eliminate "the Other" and reduce him or her to the absolute enemy, thus abrogating the trial. This, in and of itself, is an act of terrorism. Theatre emphasizes differences, not consensus; it is a place of uncertainty, of conflicting ideas. It is a space for dialogue that is open to contentious issues before an attentive audience who listens for different viewpoints and conflicting personalities. Questions and issues that revolve around human rights and freedom remain one of the main concerns and material of theatre. It has been and remains a place to tackle the subjects of censorship, freedom of expression, religion, sex, political prisoners, torture, executions, forced migrations, exile, slavery, women's rights, and child abuse, to delve into and question these subjects before a group of individuals.

The questions to explore are 'how to deal with those sensitive issues and certain causes in order to reflect on them,' how to put forward abstract ideas such as justice, freedom, humanity, punishment, and commitment without falling into the trap of formulating closed rather than comprehensive and complete concepts? No idea that claims to be perfect can be compatible with all issues that people may face in their lives. What distinguishes these abstract ideas is their ability to provide an opportunity for us to interpret them and create new concepts derived from their core. Claiming that a single concept is complete and then imposing it on a group of individuals merely annuls the concept of individual freedom and constitutes a step towards establishing a totalitarian dictatorship.

The totalitarian state, much like the security state, deals with citizens as if they are minors. The home country is administrated according to strict laws while citizens are urged to unite as a single body against external threats. As the Lebanese writer Hazem Saghieh has said, there is nothing left for this polity to do except hold demonstrations in support of the regime and chant slogans denouncing the wicked external enemy. Their anger is expressed as the anger of children, yelling and wailing their objections without listening or understanding; language breaks down, and conversation and discussion become nearly impossible.

Theatre is the public space created by the city. It is where discussions, pleadings, and the presentation of ideas take place. Today, it seems to me that theatre cannot operate except in a state based on institutions and rule of law that regulates relations between members of the community, protects citizens and their rights from encroachment, and prevents any individual, no matter how high his or her position, from becoming unrivalled in power.

Theatre needs an audience made up of individual citizens who enjoy civil rights as well as the right of choice and freedom of expression, who have the time to think and meditate, and who each have at least two spheres, including a private life which differentiates him or her from other individuals and a public one that gathers them together. It is theatre's duty to deal with the audience as a group of individual citizens and not a monolithic block, of one color and one voice, that thinks as one. The theatre practitioner must be aware of the danger of anticipating the makeup of the audience, of trying to imagine beforehand their tastes, opinions, and reactions. It is a condition of the theatre that we enter as strangers. A stranger is one who has left his or her homeland and community. A stranger is also unfamiliar. The familiar is that to which we have grown accustomed, that which makes us comfortable, and it is lethal to theatre.

Theatre is like exile. It is not a place for comfort, nor is it a place of custom or worship; it is discovery, research, and the arrangement of new relationships. Theatre is life in the anguish of exile.

I long for a theatre that makes me feel like a stranger among my people, family, and friends so that I get to know them and myself anew. Theatre is the desire and the need to go beyond the limits of the space into which we were born and raised in order to return to it as strangers. It is the desire to escape in order to meet "the Other," the desire to discover the unknown, to expand borders and erase lines, lines between "here" and "there," between the "I" and the "you," between the individual and the community, and between East and West.

Saadallah Wannous told us that we are doomed by hope, but he did not specify which hope would spell our doom. Is it the hope of theatre that sparks dialogue and provides pleasure in the city? Or is it the hope of the restoration of civil society as the guardian of theatre in the city? Is it faith in 'a culture that helps restore to people their humanity?' What city, people, and theatre are we talking about?

What has slipped away is so far, and what is yet to come so close ...

Despite the complexity and challenges of revolution, it is no longer impossible in our region. The time has come when it is more possible than ever. Indeed, 'we are doomed by hope. Come what may, today' in the Arab world proves Wannous's point, that 'today cannot be the end of history,' that it never falls under one man's sovereignty.

Translated by Meris Lutz

Note

1. Text in single quotation marks in this essay is taken from Saadallah Wannous, *al-Ightisab* [Rape] (Beirut: Dar Al Adab, 1990) and Saadallah Wannous, "al-Jou ila al-Hiwar" [Thirst for Dialogue] (1996 World Theatre Day address), in *al-Aamal al-Kamilah* [The Complete Works] (Damascus: Al Ahali, 1996), 1:39–44.

12

Shakespeare, Global Debris, and International Political Theatre

Sulayman Al Bassam

> Ensemble: This is a tale.
> Actor 5: And we are actors.
> Actor 3: We performed it so that, together with you, we would learn from it.
> Actor 7: Do you now know why elephants exist?
> Actress 3: Do you now know why elephants breed?
> Actor 5: Yet our tale is only the beginning.
> Actor 4: When elephants breed, a new tale begins.
> Ensemble: A bloody, violent tale ... A tale to perform, all of us together, when next we meet.[1]

Thus speak the actors to the audience in the final moments of *The Elephant, the King of All Time* (1969) by Saadallah Wannous. In this allegory, the King's pet elephant that stomps the life out of village children functions as a metaphor for violent political oppression. Now, more than four decades later, the "new tale" that Wannous imagined, the tale in which we are all actors, the consolation, the vindication has come.

The clocks that stood as still as coffins ticked again, releasing the living and avenging the wronged. The portraits that Doomsday itself could not have unhooked from public buildings, hotel lobbies, theatre arches, and tobacconists shops were ripped from walls and stamped underfoot. The specimen jar the Arab world floated in, like a nineteenth-century homunculus, fell onto the floor of history and smashed. A door was opened, something new and totally other entered the stage, and its name was "Spring." Spring came because the young outnumber the old; because the young, though literate, do not fear death; and because whips, bullets, and torture chairs can only suppress ignominy, hunger, and rage for so long. The world as Wannous knew it – though he'd seen revolutions before – has changed, utterly altered.

When Wannous departed this world in 1997, I was making work in Europe, grappling with the living legacies of Peter Brook, Robert Wilson, and Frank Castorf; intrigued by Romeo Castellucci, Forced Entertainment, Tadeusz Kantor, Lev Dodin; and nonplussed by new British realism. I wanted to make trouble for the great tradition of European theatre. In 1997, what did I care about the challenges facing the Arab dramatist? I was a London-based theatre maker, engaging with post-modern Europe, blissfully insouciant of my alienness.

It wasn't until the magnesium flash of 9/11 that I saw that alienness. In the fallout of the terrorist attacks on Manhattan, lines were drawn into cities and ethnicities across the Western world. Overnight, my looks, my language, my name became sources of interrogation and suspicion. I was poised between two cultures with a sense of identity defined as much by non-assimilation and non-belonging as by any unified narrative of tribe, culture, language, or history. I began to make tentative descriptions of the Arab world, in English, presenting this work in Kuwait, in Tunis, in London: I was being drawn back in. By the time I presented the first, fully conceived version of *The Al Hamlet Summit* at the Edinburgh Festival in the summer of 2002, I was already back living in Kuwait, where the convoys of US tanks were lining up in preparation for the impending invasion/liberation of Iraq.

I had rejoined the Arab world and found myself in a place where the logic of linear time could hide – and remain hidden! Despite having broached the new millennium, time went into darker and darker swirls, and for more than a decade, it seemed that time in the Arab world was moving, not forwards, but backwards. We re-entered the age of the crusades: we found ourselves in the age of jihadist warriors, messianic discourse, book burning, witch hunting, and bloodthirsty demagogy.

The spectacular destruction of the Twin Towers spawned a twin-headed serpent. The ideological poisons of neoconservatism and Salafi jihadism fused into a gargantuan and terrible beast. The beast devoured words, bodies, nations, enflaming sectarian tensions and scorching the very earth that might have sheltered dialogue between neighbors, communities, civilizations. In the vacuum created by the collapse of the Twin Towers, the Arab-Islamic world was sucked into the global arena.

From the fallout of 9/11 came global debris: the War on Terror, the invasions of Afghanistan and Iraq, the Israeli Apartheid Wall, Al Qaeda in Mesopotamia, the Danish Cartoons Episode, and more. Local events, perfectly analyzable in their local contexts, were hyperbolized and refracted around the earth via global news networks, creating inexplicable and uncontrollable fallout. More than ever, experience as lived and experience as relayed were overlapping. The virtual and the real were intersecting: globalization was becoming part of our genes, our fate, our continuum.

Nonetheless, like the Sleepers in the Cave,[2] the governments and rulers of the Arab world persisted, unperturbed, in their earthly slumbers. By the end of the first decade of the new millennium, it seemed that the Arab world had reached the nadir of time. The combined age of the heads of state of the countries of the Arab League rivaled the historical age of Islam itself; so-called republics were being fattened up and handed from father to son like golden calves.[3] Decades of cronyism, authoritarianism, Western opportunism, and administrative corruption seem to have led to an irrevocable brain drain and an irreversible shredding of the fabric of tolerance within Arab societies.

Bad times for living: rich pickings for theatre.

* * *

From this global debris, I sought to create theatre. The work I made fell into various categories and brought me into dialogue with different authors. I worked with Heiner Müller and the British dramatist Torben Betts to find a response to the invasion of Iraq. I worked on Molière's *Tartuffe* while satirizing religious hypocrisy in Gulf society. I worked on iconic figures from Islamic history like Ibn Al Muqaffa to find ways of dramatizing the impulse that drives societies towards sectarian bloodbaths. The most ambitious and consequent of these projects has been the Shakespearean cycle of works.

These pieces, which began as individual projects, each employ a Shakespeare text as a point of departure, and over time – unconsciously at first and then with increased self-awareness – became an interrelated and unified body of work. *The Al Hamlet Summit*; *Richard III, an Arab Tragedy*; and *The Speaker's Progress*, collectively framed as the Arab Shakespeare Trilogy, were all made out of the events and currents that informed the period between 2001 and 2011. The trilogy is a progeny of the globalized era, and rather than allowing that lineage to eliminate dialogue and annihilate meaning, I, alongside a dedicated and talented team of collaborators, strove to transform the condition of globalization into a liberating architecture in which to actualize a new form of Arab political theatre. Through a mixture of necessity, chance, and design, the plays in this trilogy were developed through international collaborations and partnerships that consciously implicated the resultant productions in the economy – and politics – of global culture.[4]

It was as an outsider to the intricacies of theatre production in the Arab world that I accepted the invitation of a Japanese arts organization to remake *The Al Hamlet Summit* in Arabic. A representative of the Tokyo International Arts Festival had seen the piece, in its English form, at the Cairo International Festival of Experimental Theatre (CIFET) in 2002. Two years later, as the Japanese army entered the southern Iraqi city of Samawa in the highly controversial first deployment of troops beyond Japanese soil since the Second World War, we premiered the work in Tokyo under festival slogans that read: "Social revitalization of theatre," "Reconciliation of cultural globalism and multiculturalism," and "Understanding Islamic culture."[5]

At the intersection of global politics and cultural policy, where many of the opportunities to make my international work emerged, little is random. At the time, however, I felt like Oedipus at Davlia, the unwitting protagonist at a junction of convergent paths. These paths gave me the opportunity to form a company of actors, artists, and technicians from a variety of Arab and non-Arab nationalities, thereby overcoming the first obstacle that stands in the way of contemporary Arab theatre practice: namely, nationalism.

Cultural policy-makers in the Arab world are deeply suspicious of anything that allows artists to create work beyond the yoke of the state. The artist is best contained within the stocks and gallows of state funding and state censorship. Any practice that loosens the leash of the state around artists' necks is fiercely resisted by the mechanism of state art production. Pan-Arab – dare I conjure its demons? – transnational, non-governmental artistic collaborations are suspect and undesirable by definition. The absurd pinnacle of the artistic straightjacket of state nationalism is a type of inter-Arab state festival in which Ministers of Culture (or Information!) from around the Arab world respond to invitations from their counterparts to send representative envoys of theatrical art to compete in festivals that distribute hotel rooms, meal vouchers, and prizes on the basis of nation-state identity. Troupes performing at Les Journées Théâtrales de Carthage, Cairo's CIFET, the Damascus, Amman, Kuwait, and Sharjah Festivals are invited, not on the basis of their artistic merit, but rather as representatives of their country. The yoke of the state is omnipresent.[6]

Separately, on a purely practical artistic level, in order to find the actors with sufficient range, expressive ability, and experience to create the work I envisioned, I needed to look beyond the boundaries of one state. The three plays that make up the trilogy explore in their own different ways a thematically connected body of issues: power, corruption, radical ideologies, and the forces that move societies towards fracture, dissolution or – as is the case in *The Speaker's Progress* – major change. The plays deal with issues that are systemic to more than one Arab society. As a result, they consciously seek to position themselves outside the contingencies of localized, national politics and within a more universal framework of regional concerns.

Given this content, it is difficult to imagine any Arab state willing to produce and disseminate this work. Indeed, as the trilogy developed and performed internationally and as new co-producers were sought to fund the creation of new works in the cycle, it proved impossible to find support from any Arab state-funding mechanism. The global, international interface of theatre production was, therefore, instrumental in unhooking and liberating my work from the stifling contingencies of parochial, state-based artistic practice. However, the international framework of production also brings with it its own limitations, its own curse.

The agenda instigated by international co-production is to create a work for an international audience, a dramatic work fit for "export," fit for global consumption, anytime, anywhere, whereas the aim of the Arab Shakespeare Trilogy has always been to catalyze a process of change within the Arab world. The two objectives are, it would seem, divergent.

More critically, in presenting our work on the international stage, there was always the danger of falling into the trap of Orientalism. Within a globalized media landscape that portrays the Arab world and its peoples in negative stereotypical forms as the pre-modern, sensualist, bloodthirsty, irrational Other (the Calibans!), there was a constant risk that the content of the material I was presenting – obsessed as it often is by violence, death, corruption, and irrationality – be hijacked, misunderstood, and used to reinforce a status quo based on prejudice, ignorance, and hatred. It took me some time to work out the most effective strategies to address these issues, and throughout the ten-year period, different solutions were adopted for each project. What these various strategies and devices shared was the intention to establish a double-edged moral critique within the mechanisms of the plays themselves.

As outlined above, the pieces are highly critical of dominant political practices inside the Arab world; however, they simultaneously construct a second political discourse that is directed towards audiences outside the Arab world, looking in. The result of this double-edged moral thrust is that neither Arab audiences nor their Western counterparts can watch these pieces without feeling a sense of being addressees in a dramatic political dialogue that elicits engagement.

Audience expectation and audience recognition play important roles in this. I have written elsewhere about the utility of Shakespeare as a decoy to get beyond local taboo structures and censorship.[7] Theatre makers operating under censorship have long adopted the mask of the world classic to make pointed critique of their societies without exposing themselves directly to censure and punishment. A second crucial aspect of working with and from Shakespearean texts is to understand the baggage they bring with them. By "baggage," I refer to what the Shakespearean texts represent on an iconic, cultural, and theatrical level as a result of their accrued performance and critical histories. *Hamlet*, for instance, has become shorthand for existential trauma; *Richard III*, shorthand for evil. These auxiliary meanings – the baggage – figure strongly in the minds of audiences coming to see these pieces and form part of the associative awareness that audiences bring to a performance. They act as lures that tempt audiences into the piece in anticipation of experiencing the pleasure afforded by recognition. The Shakespearean baggage, therefore, is very much part of the performance before the show even begins and influences how I am led to adapt, construct, and present the piece.

Arab audiences coming to see Shakespeare in Arabic expect to see a romantic tale set in far-away castles that has import to them primarily through the veil of allegory. The Shakespearean character names maintained in the texts feed this audience anticipation and consolidate it in order to better subvert it through the urgent sense of contemporaneity created by the language, costumes, style, and content of the piece. Audiences recognize the allegorical veil that they anticipated, but when that veil is shredded, Arab audiences become the addressees of highly realistic, contemporary political drama.

Western or non-Arab audiences come expecting the reverse: to see a familiar tale made distant and novel through its ethnographic re-coloring into Arabic. There is an inherent exoticism in the Western audience's expectations of these pieces. In a strategy similar to that used with Arab audiences, the plays transform Western audiences into addressees of dramatic political discourse by recognizing and reinforcing their expectations on one level, while challenging and subverting them on another. The plays use the familiar tropes of the Shakespearean tale – the character names, the storyline – not to tell the Shakespearean story but rather to challenge the audience's own preconceptions about the "Arab world" and, furthermore, its issues, their causes, and the postcolonial discourse that informs the relationship of the West to the Arab world.

An example of this is Margaret's monologue that opens *Richard III, an Arab Tragedy*:

> Margaret: I am Margaret. You needn't be concerned about me; we lost. It is your right to ignore me. I would ignore myself if my history let me. I don't want your loans, your gifts, your reconstruction grants; I don't want your pity – we lost. All I ask from you is not to question my thirst for revenge. It's not because I'm Arab; I read history and see. In all

> events, my name is not Margaret, but our history is
> so awful even the victors have changed their names.[8]

Margaret employs her Shakespearean name but immediately qualifies it by defining herself as the marginalized, defeated, exoticized Other. She establishes a logic of conquest in which she, Margaret, is posited as the vanquished, and the unsuspecting audience is thrust into the role of the victor. Then, in a reversal of victim psychology, she attacks the condescending assumptions of the victor's gaze and defines its parameters. She confounds the voices of the Shakespearean Margaret (the defeated, punished, outcast Lancastrian ex-Queen) with the underlying narrative position of Arab performer addressing a hegemonic (Western) audience. She also prepares the viewers for the ensuing game of subtextual meaning that will be played beneath the banner of Shakespearean nameplates and the ethnographic curio that is Shakespeare in Arabic. In this way, through an acute and explicit self-awareness of the stakes involved in presenting intercultural political theatre, the pieces seek to engage with the expectations and prejudices of non-Arab audiences in order to entangle them in a programmatic subversion of their own prejudices.

As we toured these works internationally to mostly non-Arabophone audiences, it became increasingly clear that audiences were apprehending the work as much through the supertitle screens that hung above the stage as through the stage action and stage pictures. This rather primitive observation led me to begin incorporating the supertitles themselves into the range of artistic devices available to the performance. The general rule with supertitles is that they should be as utilitarian as possible, providing a link of comprehension: they should not try to do more than they can do and certainly should never intentionally try to confuse the audience or draw attention away from the main event.

During the tour of *Richard III, an Arab Tragedy* through a variety of host languages (and late nights with translators), I began to play with these rules and, from performance to performance, would edit and embellish supertitle slides with an aim not to clarify meaning but, at times, to obscure it. The next stage of this treatment of supertitles would have been to transform the letters and projections themselves into visual elements that work outside the frame of the supertitle screen and get projected onto the stage, the set, the frame of the proscenium, the bodies of the actors, and so on. This was something we talked a lot about with the design team but never had the time or means to explore properly.

In this process of playing with the rules of live supertitling, the role of the Anglophone characters in the plays became very important. Within each of these Arabic-language pieces, there are small but consequent roles written with English dialogue.[9] When these roles are activated and the language of performance switches into English, there is an immediate and tangible engagement on the part of the non-Arabophone audiences with the live action on stage. Language is suddenly liberated from its foreignness and thrust into unmediated instancy. It is the theatrical equivalent of the cinematic zoom, and non-Arab audiences engage and identify with the Anglophone actor physiologically, almost despite themselves.

Inevitably, however, there are limits to the success of these strategies. There are limits to what can be achieved with text-driven work presented primarily to theatre audiences who do not share the same language and cultural references. *The Al Hamlet Summit*, for example, was a play about a region.[10] The piece, which was experimental in its form, acting styles, and radical reappropriation of the Shakespearean text, revolved around the concerns of a vast and multifarious region. Though littered with specifics of place and time ("Merkava tanks on the border … Shia rebels in the South"), the play never named its setting. In its staging, costumes, language, and imagery, the piece intentionally avoided defining its allegorical referent in order to maintain an interpretive openness, which allowed audiences to fill in the gaps. This interpretive openness was at times cumbersome and counterproductive as audiences – and critics – often lacked the required degree of knowledge about the Arab region to fill in the gaps. As a result, there were shows when it felt like the piece served to reaffirm general impressions of an over-stereotyped region without enabling audiences to get beyond their ignorance.[11]

We learn as we go along.

Sculpting audience and critical perception of international political theatre is, to a large degree, a shared remit. It is the joint responsibility of the makers of the work, on the one hand, and the international presenting partners, on the other, who receive, market, and sell the work. Space does not permit me to go into the intricacies of this, but suffice to say that in our tours, we have been both blessed and challenged in this regard.

* * *

We had played in the Far East, we had played in the Far West, we had dealt with their expectations and challenged them. We had played to Princesses and Presidents;[12] we had surprised others and ourselves. Western counterparts, it transpires, are also looking for something within contemporary Arab theatre beyond the purely topical. The West is entering into a period of post-supremacy and economic decline in which it can sense the end of its structures of dominance. Within the work of Arab theatre makers, perhaps, they are able to find a mirror of themselves, beyond the ethnographic other: if we are the Calibanized Other, note well that Prospero's staff is hollow.

As I moved to make the *The Speaker's Progress*, it made sense that the final piece in the trilogy be produced by an Arab co-producer and that the play open, first and foremost, in the Arab world. This piece, I told myself, will be different. This time, it will take inspiration not from a Shakespearean portrait of carnage, not from a blood fest, but from a comedy, *Twelfth Night*.[13] But when negotiations with Gulf funders collapsed and no other Arab funding bodies were interested, I found myself asking: who is this for? Where is this work's audience? What possible difference can this theatre project make to the Arab world when it is hardly permissible to perform inside the Arab world? What is the utility in theatre when it cannot be delivered to its intended audience?

This spirit of disillusion and bitterness fueled the development of the concluding piece in the trilogy. I should clarify that I had not known this body of work would end as a trilogy, but I had reached a point of suffusion with Shakespeare and had a formal and artistic need for closure that made the idea of a trilogy appear both inevitable and right. So, in *The Speaker's Progress*, a retired theatre director, assuming the fatal pretense of a regime apologist, attempts a last roll of the dice. It features a portrait of a theatre maker – myself – gasping for air inside a system that, through method and indifference, had succeeded in forcing the oxygen out of individual and popular imaginations. Then, in an ironic volte-face of history, while rehearsing this piece in Damascus, a door opened, something new and totally other entered the stage: Spring.

On January 4, 2011, Mohammed Bouazizi, the Tunisian physicist-fruit-seller, dies from the burns of his self-inflicted auto-da-fé. The image of his act, his body, his funeral, the state snipers, the swelling masses, the rise of the chanting tide – all pitched and tossed from phone to phone, screen to screen, tweet to tweet, terminal to terminal, city to city; Cairo, then Yemen, the East of Libya, Manama, the South of Syria: here was the end of hidden time, time resurfacing, time again. Millions took to the streets to reclaim their dignity. Dictators fled their palaces, were committed to hospitals, or put under siege. Arab history rejoined the living. The debris of old systems crumbling and new systems erupting continues to spume, swirl, fall.

So now, after all these years of resistance through making theatre about things that end badly, there's a need to make space for euphoria. We feel an urgent need to change the ending, even while acknowledging that euphoria must be lived first, before it can be staged. During the preview performances of *The Speaker's Progress* in Kuwait in late February 2011, there was something hugely liberating about being swept up in the euphoria that consumed the Arab world. But the signification and dramatic language of these upheavals needs more thought. What has been happening since January 2011 has made way for many alternatives to the traditional ideas of power and people, and even the relationship between writing and reality. Endings should no longer be endings: they are beginnings. Suddenly, there is so much life to be lived, so much that demands imagining and re-imagining. It is in that re-imagining that Arab theatre needs to embrace its aesthetic and civic responsibilities to help shape an ethics of the post-revolutionary imagination.

I concluded *The Speaker's Progress* with a proposition which I firmly believe: that the light shed by the events of the Arab Revolutions demands new texts, new ways of imagining. Critique uttered from behind Shakespearean masks, the masks of others, is no longer a valid critique for this phase of Arab drama, this moment of Arab history. The awakenings have shattered the mirrors and the masks.

It is, therefore, by a sweet turn of fate that – at the time of writing – I find myself invited to direct Saadallah Wannous's play, *Ritual for a Metamorphosis* (1994), at La Comédie Française in Paris in 2013. This production will be the first Arabic text to enter into the repertoire of that august institution in its long, venerable history. It is the start of a new journey for me that opens with the championing of a seminal Arabic text inside the very heart of European theatrical tradition. There is an element of poetic justice in this – just a slither, a splinter, a passing sadness, a farewell to Shakespeare. There is something about it that reminds me of the magical and melancholy transformation charted in Shakespeare's Sonnet 29:

> When, in disgrace with fortune and men's eyes,
> I all alone beweep my outcaste state
> ...
> For thy sweet love remember'd such wealth brings
> That then I scorn to change my state with kings.[14]

Notes

1. Saadallah Wannous, *al-Fil ya Malik al-Zaman* [The Elephant, the King of All Time], in *al-Aamal al-Kamilah* [The Complete Works] (Damascus: Al Ahali, 1996), 1:578–9. Translation by the editor.
2. Sleepers in the Cave (*Ahl al-Kahf*) is the Muslim equivalent of the Seven Sleepers tale, in which a group of brothers fall asleep in a cave for three centuries. See the Quran, Surah 18, *al-Kahf*.
3. The golden calf is a symbol of pagan idolatry according to the Book of Exodus and the Quran, Surah 20, *Ta Ha*.
4. Elements of this essay are rooted in conversations with Professor Margaret Litvin conducted and recorded in Beirut, Lebanon in May 2011. I am grateful for her time and generous contribution to the process of reflecting upon the work and also to Professor Graham Holderness, who instigated the Beirut conversation.
5. See Nobuko Tanaka, "International Theatre Festival Takes Japan to a New Stage," *Japan Times*, February 24, 2004, www.japantimes.co.jp/text/ft20040225a1.html.
6. The Kuwaiti state refused to recognize *The Al Hamlet Summit* as a sufficiently worthy state export. Thus, it was performed at CIFET in 2002 as a representative of the United Kingdom, where the producing company, Zaoum Theatre, was based. The piece was awarded the top accolades of Best Director and Best Performance Awards.
7. See Sulayman Al Bassam, "The Bard of Basra," *Guardian* (London), September 22, 2005.

8. Sulayman Al Bassam, *Richard III, an Arab Tragedy*, in *L'avant scène théâtre*, 1244 (2008): 14.
9. In *The Al Hamlet Summit*, the English-language role was The Arms Dealer. In *Richard III, an Arab Tragedy*, the English-language role was The American Ambassador Richmond. In *The Speaker's Progress* and in non-Arab venues only, the English-language role is The Speaker.
10. See Sulayman Al Bassam, *The Al Hamlet Summit* (Hertfordshire: University of Hertfordshire Press, 2006).
11. See, for example, Peter Culshaw, "Shakespeare and Suicide Bombers," *Daily Telegraph* (London), March 1, 2004.
12. In May 2008, Syrian President Bashar Al Assad attended the final performance of *Richard III, an Arab Tragedy* in Damascus. In April 2009, the same play performed to a private audience of female members of the ruling family in the United Arab Emirates. For more insight into this, see the documentary film *Richard III: An Arab VIP*, directed by Shakir Abal and Tim Langford (Kuwait: The Culture Project, 2010).
13. The idea to use *Twelfth Night* as the play-within-a-play of *The Speaker's Progress* was suggested by the co-conceiver of piece, Georgina Van Welie.
14. William Shakespeare, *The Complete Works* (New York: Barnes & Noble, 2005), 1228.

13

The Things I am Afraid to Tell You: Performing Palestine in Diaspora

Joseph Shahadi

The theatre of Palestine is, for a variety of reasons,[1] under-studied. In her essay "Stories From Under Occupation: Performing the Palestinian Experience," Hala Kh. Nassar introduces Palestinian theatre in its historical context by considering what makes it distinct from other Arab theatres. She argues that "by generating hybrid cultural productions under military occupation, Palestinian theatre exemplifies postcolonial experiences precisely because of this struggle to (re)create a national identity."[2] However, she does not extend her inquiry to include the theatre of the Palestinian Diaspora. If, as Nassar suggests, one use of the theatre in Palestine is to remake Palestinian identity through performance, we might ask how far the unifying effects of this theatrical strategy may stretch into Diaspora.

Palestinian-American theatre artists like actress/playwrights Najla Said, Lameece Isaaq, and Betty Shamieh, playwright/performance poets Ismail Khalidi and Remi Kanazi, and comedians Maysoon Zaid and Dean Obeidallah, co-founders of the New York Arab-American Comedy Festival, all explore themes related to Palestinian identity in their work. Artists such as these provide a unique view into the dynamic between performance, nationalism, and the occupation of Palestine by staging identity in a diasporic context. In this essay, I'd like to begin a larger conversation about the characteristics of theatre in the Palestinian Diaspora by foregrounding one such performance, Jennifer Jajeh's solo *I Heart Hamas: And Other Things I am Afraid to Tell You.*[3]

In the dark before her show begins, a businesslike voice-over by Palestinian-American actress and playwright Jennifer Jajeh fills the space:

> Good evening ladies and gentleman. Welcome to "I Heart Hamas: And Other Things I'm Afraid to Tell You," a tragicomic solo show written and performed by Jennifer Jajeh. Tonight's show will run approximately one and a half hours with a ten-minute intermission. Before we begin, Jennifer has asked that the audience observe the following rules:
>
> For the next 90 minutes, Jennifer would like you to consider the current conflict in the Middle East from the Palestinian perspective.
>
> No audience member will deny Jennifer's existence in particular tonight or the existence of Palestinians in general.
>
> Jennifer will not be representing the views or feelings of the "average Palestinian," nor does she have any idea what that even means.
>
> After the show, please do not engage Jennifer in unsolicited political discussions, disputes or disagreements. (*Pause*) But you may buy her a drink.
>
> To all of the Arab and Palestinian audience members: You are asked to refrain from pointing out that Jennifer's Arabic sucks, and please do not ask her age or why she is not yet married.
>
> To all of the Jewish and Israeli audience members: Relax, the show isn't about you. It's about Jennifer ...[4]

And so begins Jajeh's solo performance, chronicling her move from San Francisco to Ramallah and back again against the backdrop of the Second Intifada. From the first moment, she establishes the wry tone of her performance by conflating the ordinary instructions to theatrical audiences (i.e. silence cell-phones, etc.) with explicit directions not to question the existence of the performer who is about to enter. This bizarre existential crisis, which flows from Golda Meir's famous Zionist dictum, "There is no such thing as a Palestinian people,"[5] is unique to Palestinians who are in the strange position of continually proving that they indeed exist. But noting the surreal dilemma caused by Meir's failed performative utterance[6] – the linguistic equivalent of covering one's eyes and proclaiming oneself invisible – allows Jajeh to dispense with it before her performance begins and makes very clear the limits of her patience: she is not interested in proving her own existence to her audience, who will meet her in person soon enough.

A first-generation American and native San Franciscan, Jennifer Jajeh can trace the roots of her family in Ramallah to its founding in the sixteenth century; however, she makes it clear at the outset that she rejects the role of representative Palestinian. "I am pretty clear that I am telling *a* Palestinian story – that is, *my* Palestinian story, not all of them. I can't be that for Arabs, Israelis, or Americans. I can only be myself."[7] Significantly, Jajeh pitches her declaration to both the Arabs/Palestinians *and* the Jews/Israelis in her audience, anticipating the claims of both groups to her subjectivity and rejecting them before she even appears. So, from the first moments of *I Heart Hamas*, Jajeh pointedly declines to identify herself within the terms that animate the ongoing conflict in Palestine: she is neither one of the "good ones" nor "one of the 'bad' ones."

Other Arab diasporic artists have explored Orientalist stereotypes in their work, critiquing the identities they suggest by embodying them and/or giving them voice. Betty Shamieh's *Chocolate in Heat: Growing Up Arab in America* (2003) and *The Black Eyed* (2007) or Laila Farah's Scheherazade *Don't Need No Visa*[8] (2002) are a few examples. But Jajeh's refusal to represent anyone other than herself means waving aside the repertoire of righteous victims and "savage" fanatics[9] that populate the discourse around the Middle East, a transgressive gesture for Arabs in the West in general, and for Palestinians, who are so often cast as characters in various national dramas, in particular. If this strategy distinguishes Jajeh's work from theatre created within Palestine and that of other Arab diasporic artists, it is atypical for solo performances in the US tradition as well.

Women, various ethnic and racial minority groups, the disabled, and queer artists have all used solo performance to stage the revolutionary potential of self-representation in relation to a majority.[10] However, these performances are often driven by the self-presentation of bodies marked by difference. Esther Kim Lee, writing about Asian American solo performance, argues that the "perpetual foreigner and stranger" must explain herself onstage. Drawing parallels to disabled artists, she writes "'The body-in-view' demands to be narrated for and against the expectations of the majority,"[11] a theatrical gesture that Jajeh refuses.

Theatrically clever *and* politically bracing, her pre-performance assertions raise an inevitable question: is it possible for Jennifer Jajeh to perform her individual "Palestinian-ness" without an explicit relationship to a larger Palestinian people or to an Israeli narrative that positions "Palestinian" as its "always already" opposite number? This question, which arises before she even emerges on stage, establishes the terrain of her diasporic Palestinian performance, frames my inquiry into her work, and gestures toward the complexity endemic to performing Palestinian identities.

Jajeh confronts the freighted assumptions she must manage in her daily life by externalizing – not embodying – them in an ongoing bit she titles "Ask a Palestinian," which runs like a spine through her performance. The stage, which is otherwise spare, features a signboard that lights up to signal incoming questions from audience members. Jajeh explains, "Okay, this is how this works. When you have a question you have to think real hard about it, and when enough of you are thinking the same question a light goes off alerting me, at which point the question will be automatically beamed into my brain and I'll decide whether or not to stop the show and answer your question."[12] The signboard then lights up with comic speed, indicating that the audience are all wondering the same things one right after another in a flurry of questions:

> (*ASK A P.* [Palestinian] *light flashes*) Already? Okay. But let's take it slow. I mean, we just met. Like a first date. (*Take out wine*) Yes, I am actually first generation.
> (*ASK A P. light*) Eww, no. There will be no belly dancing in the show tonight. It's not that kind of show.
> (*ASK A P. light*) What's my name? It's Jennifer. (*ASK A P. light*) What's my real name? Jennifer. (*Pause*) No. I don't have an "Arabic" name. (*ASK A P. light*) No. Really. It's Jennifer Ann Catherine. (*Pause*) No, that's not a weird name for a Palestinian: there are Palestinians with all sorts of horrible names like Tiffany and Heather and Amber and Melanie.
>
> My middle name is Ann because my dad had a thing for a woman named Ann, which is really creepy if you think about it, and I can't believe my mom let him get away with that. And Catherine is my confirmation name. (*Pause.*)
> (*ASK A P. light*) Yes, confirmation. The Sacrament. I'm Christian. Catholic actually. (*ASK A P. light*) No, we didn't convert? Of course there are Christians in Palestine. It's the Holy Land. The birthplace of Jesus. You know, Jesus? The founder of the Christian faith? Yeah, well Jesus was born in Palestine, as was my mom. If you think abut it, Palestinians are actually the original Christians. We've been onboard this Christianity train since the get go. So I don't know why it's become all about the pope and the Italians, born again Christians and televangelists. We were Christians when they were still living in caves ...[13]

Of course, Jajeh the author is really "answering" herself here, although these are typical of the questions she faces as a matter of routine. And she is not choosing to "stop" the show to answer them: answering them *is* the show. But by rendering the askers mute via theatrical conceit, rather than portraying them herself as she does elsewhere, she gives the audience an opportunity to experience them from her point of view.

Jajeh has said that one of her explicit reasons for writing the show was to "get it all out at one time, and answer all of these stupid questions at once ... and be done with them."[14] But I'd suggest it is her frustration at their shallow temerity that is being staged rather than the questions themselves, or their answers. In other words, rather than simply challenging Palestinian stereotypes and providing a corrective for the benefit of her audience, which is the theme of many of the (largely positive) reviews of her work,[15] it is her anger at being forced to constantly explain herself that is central to her performance.

Jajeh's anger, which flashes through her witty text, resonates through the absurd scenarios she stages. For example, in another scene, the thirty-something Jajeh lampoons her single status – a source of frustration to her Arab relatives and strangers alike – by announcing that she is in a loving relationship with her cat, Judah. Judah, whose previous owner was the deceased mother of a friend, was originally meant to stay with her temporarily, an arrangement that settled into permanence after a year. Nevertheless, before agreeing to permanently relinquish his mother's cat to Jajeh, her friend David, who is Jewish, insists on checking with his relatives in Israel. After weighing in from afar, they agree that the Palestinian Jajeh may keep the cat as long as she does not change his name because it "reflects his Jewish identity." The scene – with Jajeh playing both herself and "David" – is absurdly funny. (The Palestinian clerk at the corner store where she buys cat food, also portrayed by Jajeh, suggests giving the cat a "good Arabi name. Like Nimer.") But the scene ends with an incredulous Jajeh telling off her friend:

> His Jewish identity? Are you serious? Should I get him circumcised? Do we have to start celebrating Hanukkah? Should I take him to synagogue? This is totally ridiculous David. It's not like I was gonna

> change his name anyway. I thought we were friends. I can't believe you of all people would try to pull this crazy Jewish-Israeli-Palestinian shit on me. What exactly are you afraid I'm going to do to him? Change his name to Mohammad? Turn him into a militant, Hamas kitty? You realize there is a war, and people are being killed and oppressed and tortured. And you want to fight over a cat? A cat you don't even want. A cat you abandoned. This cat is not an extension of your fucking identity. And by the way a cat can't be Jewish.[16]

For Jajeh, who describes her show as "tragicomic," the ridiculousness of this situation, which she mines for its humor, does not diminish the pain it causes her. And her contempt for the grotesque extremes that Israeli-Palestinian identity politics provoke is clear. Against her (considerable) will, she lives in a world where something as prosaic as cat ownership is burdened with implications about identity, both hers and that of people she has never met.

Theatre within Palestine has also acted as a vehicle for the complex anger of its makers, but the difference in the causes and uses of that anger are instructive and further illuminate the dynamics suggested by Jajeh's performance. While theatre has nearly always been a part of Palestinian city life,[17] it is the theatre created under Israeli occupation that inspires the greatest scholarly interest.[18] As with Britain before it, Israel confounds political expressions from the Palestinian people; however, unlike the comparatively stable British mandate, the Israeli definition of "political" is widely variable and far ranging. "Censorship battles are waged over the symbolic value of anything that can be seen as part of the Palestinian cultural repertoire ... whose existence [is] metonymic ... of Palestinian identity, the existence of which is officially denied."[19] So, battles over cultural production in Palestine mirror the underlying conflict of the occupation, as the Israeli colonial narrative is incompatible with the self-representation of the occupied. If the British exerted colonial control over the scope of Palestinian theatrical expressions during the British mandate,[20] then the Zionists adopted an even more aggressive stance toward indigenous cultural production.

Geographer Ghazi Falah argues that, in addition to destroying most Palestinian physical landscapes in founding contemporary Israel, Zionists deconstructed Palestinian cultural topographies as well. Falah suggests that this purposeful effort to "superimpose" a modern Israeli state onto Palestine was abetted by the parallel destruction of the Palestinian cultural landscape, a strategy he links to military theorist B. H. Liddell-Hart's theory of "total war."[21] Falah writes, "Israeli authorities pursued a strategy, which, by removing the past cultural traces of other peoples from the landscape, undercut and weakened Palestinian claims to this territory, i.e., a strategy of 'de-signification' ... In this process of cultural landscape transformation, one party systematically attempted to eliminate the other's attachment to their habitat."[22] Performance studies scholar Diana Taylor has theorized the special utility of performance in maintaining the coherence of culture in a Latin American context. She writes, "Performances function as vital acts of transfer, transmitting social knowledge, memory, and a sense of identity through reiterated, or what Richard Schechner has called, 'twice-behaved behavior.'"[23]

Following Taylor's logic, a purposeful disruption of cultural production then is an act of violence against a people, enacted in the present, which erases both the past and the future. Palestinian activists and thinkers like Ghassan Kanafani and Hanan Ashrawi have argued that Palestinian cultural production, including theatre created under occupation, is a form of resistance to Israeli cultural imperialism.[24] But while theatre within Palestine is often charged with upholding the struggle by maintaining continuity with an amputated cultural tradition,[25] Jennifer Jajeh's diasporic Palestinian performance rejects this responsibility. Jajeh instead stages her repeated attempts to transcend these politics and the range of feelings they evoke in her: amusement, hurt, sadness, and anger. But her anger is personal, not communal. If the righteous anger that characterizes much of the theatre in

Palestine rebuilds ever-depleting cultural capital in the face of organized efforts to obliterate it, then Jajeh's anger opens her up to the possibility of a life beyond that struggle.

As the second act begins, Jajeh is dissatisfied with her life and career and has relocated to Palestine. She explains, prompted by the "Ask a Palestinian" signboard:

> Honestly. I don't know exactly why I came here. I felt like something was missing from my life. Nothing was working for me. It wasn't some big, finding my roots homecoming thing though. I just wasn't happy and didn't know why. It was always such a big deal to everyone else about where I came from so I figured I'd find out why ... I've met a lot of cool people my age. And everyone looks like me or one of my cousins. There's this weird feeling that everything is familiar. You know the language, the faces, the smells. It all smells like my mom's kitchen. I feel really comfortable and at home.[26] Which I wasn't really expecting. So I'm going back to the States to wrap up my life there and am moving back here. Maybe for good.[27]

Jajeh delivers this monologue against the backdrop of a party her friends in Palestine are throwing in her honor, where she is doing Tequila shots and dancing to "... Baby One More Time" by Britney Spears. The monologue confounds Western expectations about Palestine and Palestinians on multiple registers. Jajeh recasts the Palestinian homeland narrative in such casual terms that her "return" is devoid of any mythic significance. She will not commit, even in retrospect, to endowing her decision to move to Ramallah with any politics whatsoever, rendering it outside the competing Palestinian/Israeli legends that imagine unbroken continuity between people and place. Her pleasure at being there is neither spiritual nor nationalistic, but rather visceral: the familiar look of the people and homey smells of Ramallah are "weird" in their familiarity. She begins dating a local named Hakam but clarifies that she is not relocating permanently on account of him either. She says, "I don't even know if I like the guy ... He's the only guy I'm dating here. But he's just a guy, you know? I met him at the university where I'm studying Arabic. He organizes all the events for the foreign students. He's funny and sweet and persistent and I don't know, we'll see."[28]

When she returns from the United States, their relationship seems to shift, with Hakam becoming more inaccessible. We discover almost incidentally that the Second Intifada has broken out. Ramallah, which Jajeh had previously described as "pretty mellow," is changing around her. Unable to process the scope of the impact on her new life, Jajeh delivers a rare, non-narration monologue in the form of a telephone message for Hakam, who is hours late to meet her.

> Hi, it's me again. I've called you like four times. Where are you? You're two hours late. We had a date. Call me.
>
> I'm eating. That's the sound of eating in the background. I'm not waiting for you. I'm not waiting for any man. I can't believe you think it's ok to do this. Is this how you treat women here? Cuz this is totally uncool. My friends are right. You're probably just using me thinking we'll get married and I'll take you the States so you can get an American passport. Well, you know what? The passport office is officially closed.
>
> Wait, are you trying to break up with me? Is that what this is? Did you meet someone else while I was gone? I was only gone a month. Everything seems different ever since I've come back. I never see you, and with the whole Intifada thing happening, the situation here sucks, there are no parties, there's nothing to do. How did you even meet someone else, there's nowhere to go? You have a lot of explaining to do. Call me.
>
> (*Long pause*)
>
> Wait, wait, wait. Are you okay? I was pissed, and now I'm starting to get worried. Did something happen to you? Oh no, maybe something happened to you. Even if you're not coming over call me and let me know you're safe.[29]

Jajeh's comic proclamation that the intifada "sucks" because it has shut down all the parties is shocking in its self-centeredness. Her unflattering self-portrayal is unexpectedly funny, but it foreshadows the growing horror of the situation, rendering the scale of the occupation in human terms: despite Jajeh's best efforts to cling to the simple pleasures she has enjoyed in Ramallah, the grim reality of the situation intrudes. Her competing fears, that her boyfriend is using her or leaving her for someone else, which are not local to Palestine, are supplanted by the worry that he may have been killed in the uprising. In *I Heart Hamas*, comedy and horror do not cancel each other out but rather sharpen one another to an unbearable degree. Jajeh subsequently learns that Hakam had been detained in Jerusalem while buying her sushi because the Israel Defense Forces (IDF) thought the raw fish might have been a bomb. "Good thing I have the sushi," he says, "or I'd be in jail."[30]

As the intifada stretches on, the feeling of belonging Jajeh originally enjoyed is increasingly challenged, and she begins to crack beneath the pressure. At a particularly frustrating checkpoint, Jajeh spits at a departing IDF soldier, and a cheer rises up behind her:

> Suddenly, this crowd behind me starts cheering. They're cheering for me. They're cheering because I spit on the soldier. And they're saying something. What are they saying?
> (*Listens and slowly begins to chant along*) Espagnoliya. Espagnoliya. Espagnoliya? They think I'm Spanish? I'm not Spanish. (*Yelling to crowd behind me*) I'm not Spanish. I'm not Espagnoliya. I'm Palestinian, like you.[31]

The olive-skinned Jajeh, whose acting career in California had often involved portraying Latino, Hispanic, and Chicano characters – and who daydreams briefly in the first act about "becoming" Brazilian[32] – suddenly finds herself considered an outsider at this archetypal scene of encounter for a Palestinian, the checkpoint.[33] The scene is rendered absurd – or perhaps, even more absurd – by the misrecognition of the Palestinian crowd, but it is haunted by an earlier exchange she shared with an IDF soldier (the only Israeli character in the show[34]):

> What are you doing here? Hmm, making a movie? Ah, I'm in a movie now. I'm gonna be famous. What kind of movie you're making at the checkpoint? Go film something nice, like the ocean or Jerusalem. Why do you come here everyday?
>
> You like it here? She likes it here. Oh, this is your country now? What? You're Israeli now? No, this is not your country. This is my country. You're American. Go home. Get out.
>
> (*Long beat*)
>
> You know if I shoot you, nobody cares. You know that? Go. No filming today. Go.[35]

Finally, after an ever-tightening series of checkpoints and bombings, which Hakam seems to take in stride, they witness the murder of a gum-selling neighborhood boy by Israeli soldiers. The boy's death – right in front of her – proves too much for Jajeh, who soon returns "home" to the United States.

* * *

Helena Grehan describes Diaspora as both a theoretical stance and/or a condition of partial belonging, where the subject retains a link or links, however tenuous, to "an idea of 'home.'"[36] Taking up this thread, Laila Farah expands the idea to include the "schisms that occur within the diasporic person as she traverses this complicated terrain – for example, the fracturing of the concept of 'homeland' and the (sometimes forced) acculturation or assimilation that fragments identity as it was previously known."[37] In the Palestinian case, Diaspora is characterized not only by the violent fracture of physical and cultural topographies and the forced dispersal of people, but also by the ongoing experience of occupation, which supports those projects. So in the instance of Palestine, it isn't only the homeland that is occupied but also the "idea" of home. Belonging, then, in a Palestinian sense cannot simply be felt or experienced – it must be *performed.*

Jill Dolan has theorized this use of performance generally as the "utopic performative." She writes, "I find this notion very rich, the idea that in order to pretend, to enact an ideal future, a culture has to move farther and farther away from the real into a kind of performative, in which the utterance, in this case, doesn't necessarily make it so but inspires perhaps other more local 'doings' that sketch out the potential in those feignings." According to Dolan, the utopic performative is characterized by the "lucid power of intersubjective understanding, however fleeting,"[38] but it is exactly this kind of understanding that the occupation prevents. Of course the irony of utopia, which means literally "no-place," as a signifier for Palestinian performance cannot be overstated: it is the yearning for "home" that animates Palestinian cultural topographies.

While Palestinian theatre dramatizes the communal strength and creative fortitude of the Palestinian people in the face of continual violence, in *I Heart Hamas* Jennifer Jajeh stages the impossibility of that task. Grehan wonders how the body of a diasporic subject is "marked or inscribed by this journeying and how ... [s/he] inscribe[s] him/herself within/on the landscapes s/he traverses?"[39] But the overwhelming emotional, spiritual, and physical force of the occupation makes the possibility of inscription flow in only one direction; not only does the "de-signification" of Palestine serve to de-Arabize it in general terms, but the constant pressure to reinstate the Palestinian narrative consumes the cultural landscape.

Jajeh's subjectivity threatens to be swallowed up by the task. For the Palestinian-American Jajeh, the idea of "home" is fluid as she experiments with different scenarios of belonging – to her career, her boyfriend, other

Palestinian-Americans, and finally to Palestinians within Palestine itself. But these attachments suggest identities she rejects, one after another, and that refusal, which defines her freedom in the United States, hobbles her in occupied Palestine. After the murder of the gum-selling boy, she is distraught, and Hakam says to her, "Come on you have to be stronger than this if you're gonna live here," to which she responds, "I don't want to live here. I want to go home."[40] It is a meaningful acknowledgment that despite her long familial ties and current attachments there, Ramallah is not "home." Or perhaps that it isn't any longer.

In her final "Ask a Palestinian," Jajeh sums up her experience in Palestine:

> Why is the show called "I Heart Hamas?" Really? After everything I've shown you, you don't get it. Look, if I could snap, anybody could. This idea we have of what terrorism, Hamas is. That it's some mad crazy radical person. Some religious fundamentalist driven by insane motives that we can't understand. But maybe in reality, it's just a person who's had enough and doesn't see any other options. Maybe it's just a normal human reaction against oppression. After living in Ramallah for only a year and a half, I even reached a point where I could imagine blowing people up. But I had the option to leave.[41]

Finally, she admits the thing she is "afraid to tell you": that she understands the pull toward violent insurgency, that – despite disingenuous moralizing – it is not difficult to understand at all, and that, rather than proof of monstrous inhumanity, that it is the opposite, "a normal human reaction." That, finally, is the dark "heart" of *I Heart Hamas*, a performance of Jennifer Jajeh's attempt and subsequent failure to live under her own terms within occupied Palestine. And that is the story she returns to tell.

In the final scene,[42] Jajeh holds up a book that traces her family tree back to the 1500s and announces, "I am related to every single person in this book." She says:

> This is the tree of my father's family. The tree lists all of my father's ancestors. Here's my grandfather. And my dad. This is the tree of my mother's family. It goes back 15 generations. For the last 450 years my entire family line has been documented. We are the people of Ramallah, Palestine.
>
> There will never be another edition of this book because most of the people in this book fled Palestine. The history of this Christian community in Ramallah as my mom, my grandfather, my father knew it is over. I am the break in this 450-year chain, and as much as I try I can't seem to leave it behind.
>
> So tell me, where does that leave me?[43]

Jajeh's diasporic performance is not fueled by memory but rather by a total, generational break with the past, which precludes the possibility of understanding a future in its terms. Rather than performing affiliation with her family and by extension Palestine, Jajeh embodies the break in that continuity, a Palestinian identity that is uniquely diasporic. While Palestinian theatre often performs a link to a pre-1948 past (either explicitly or implicitly) and Dolan's notion of the "utopic performative" gestures, however obliquely, toward the future, Jennifer Jajeh's diasporic Palestinian performance is caught between these states of longing.

Notes

1. The occupation, of course, presents challenges to studying Palestinian cultural production, but the Palestinian theatre has traditionally not received much attention from Western or Middle Eastern scholars. See Hala Kh. Nassar, "Stories from Under Occupation: Performing the Palestinian Experience," *Theatre Journal* 58 (2006): 17. Nassar writes, "Historically, Palestine has been on the margins of such neighboring cultural centers as Beirut and Cairo. Western and Arab scholars still mention early Palestinian theatre in passing, commenting that such theatre never really developed professionally and artistically and

survives on adaptations and borrowings. When scholars do address Palestinian theatre more fully, they tend to focus only on productions after the 1967 War."

2. Nassar, "Stories," 16–17. She continues, "Operating under modern colonial rule with limited options (as it lacks original texts, actors, rehearsal spaces, and an infrastructure), Palestinian theatre has survived by embracing cultural hybridity, using patchwork as a strategy for survival. Throughout its history, Palestinian theatre has borrowed and adapted models, ideas, and methods from world drama, including Israeli theatre, in an ongoing process – in both postcolonial settings and under military occupation – of liberation and healing."
3. Jennifer Jajeh has performed *I Heart Hamas: And Other Things I am Afraid to Tell You* in theatres and at colleges and festivals all over the United States – including the New York International Fringe Festival, where I saw an early incarnation of the show – since 2008. For a comprehensive list of the show's performance history, see: I Heart Hamas: And Other Things I'm Afraid to Tell You, "Tour Dates," June 13, 2011, http://ihearthamas.com.
4. Jennifer Jajeh, "I Heart Hamas: And Other Things I am Afraid to Tell You" (unpublished playscript, 2009; rewrite, 2011), 2.
5. The complete quote reads, "There is no such thing as a Palestinian people ... It is not as if we came and threw them out and took their country. They didn't exist." Frank Giles, "Golda Meir Speaks Her Mind to Frank Giles of the London Sunday Times," *Middle East Newsletter*, June 16, 1969, A1:3.
6. The job of a performative, as theorized by linguist J. L. Austin, is to perform an action; it refers to the fact of its own successful performance. Therefore, to issue a performative utterance is to perform the action implied ("I name this ship," "I welcome you," "I apologize"). In order to be successful, a performative utterance must be made by someone qualified – the weight of her authority is necessary to effect and maintain the attendant shift in reality. That Meir did not have the authority to wish the Palestinian people out of existence with a turn of phrase is emblematic of the Palestinian perspective in the ongoing conflict. See J. L. Austin, *How to Do Things with Words*, 2nd edn. (1962; Cambridge, MA: Harvard University Press, 1975).
7. Jennifer Jajeh, interview by the author, Brooklyn, New York, June 13, 2011.
8. The Lebanese-American Farah has integrated this piece into her performance *Living in the Hyphen-Nation* (2005). She writes, "How do you know who I really am? (I manipulate the veil here from one image to the next while embodying each of the following:) the erotic/exotic harem girl, the downtrodden peasant, veiled, illiterate, miserable, squatting in the field, the *intifada* woman throwing rocks in the street, or Hanan Ashrawi paying homage at a religious site. (I perform an ululation ... long and loud ...)" Quoted in Laila Farah,

"Dancing on the Hyphen: Performing Diasporic Subjectivity," *Modern Drama*, 48, no. 2 (2005): 321–2.

9. To this list, we might add "Good Daughter," "Femme Fatale," "Harem Girl," and "Militant" among other sexist/Orientalist stereotypes.
10. For example, the solo performer Dan Kwong writes, "Telling one's story on one's own terms is an act of self-empowerment and validation, as an individual and as a member of a group. It says, 'I am here and my experience, our experience in this culture, matters.'" Dan Kwong quoted in Esther Kim Lee, "Between the Personal and the Universal: Asian American Solo Performance from the 1970s to the 1990s," *Journal of Asian American Studies*, 6, no. 3 (2003): 289.
11. Lee, "Between the Personal," 294.
12. Jajeh, "I Heart Hamas," 5.
13. Ibid.
14. Jajeh, interview.
15. For example, in their review in *People's World*, Dale Greenfield and Eric A. Gordon write, "[Jajeh] slyly but effectively and firmly dispels some of the worst stereotypes embedded in the collective American psyche regarding Palestinians." Dale Greenfield and Eric A. Gordon, "On Stage: A Palestinian American Stuck in the Middle," review of *I Heart Hamas: And Other Things I am Afraid to Tell You* by Jennifer Jajeh, *People's World*, June 16, 2011, www.peoplesworld.org/on-stage-a-palestinian-american-stuck-in-the-middle.
16. Jajeh, "I Heart Hamas," 13–14.
17. From the early medieval period, Arab and European travelers and writers noted indigenous dramatic representations in Palestine. See Susan Slyomovics, "'To Put One's Fingers in the Bleeding Wound': Palestinian Theatre under Israeli Censorship," *The Drama Review*, 35, no. 2 (1991): 22.
18. Nassar, "Stories," 17.
19. Slyomovics, "Bleeding Wound," 28.
20. Palestinian theatre under the British mandate was shaped by British taste (for imported productions) and proscriptions (against plays with political content); however, despite strict censorship, in the 1930s an explicit political consciousness emerged in local productions. This budding awareness was configured against the interference of outside forces in Palestine, represented locally by the British mandate and in a larger sense by growing Zionist designs on the region. See Nassar, "Stories," 17.
21. Ghazi Falah writes, "The act of expulsion [of the Palestinian people] is conceptualized as part of an Israeli strategy of 'total war' that targeted both Palestinian civilian population and their landscapes." See Ghazi Falah, "The 1948 Israeli-Palestinian War and its Aftermath: The Transformation and De-

Signification of Palestine's Cultural Landscape," *Annals of the Association of American Geographers*, 86, no. 2 (1996): 256. The term "total war," as theorized by military strategist B. H. Liddell-Hart, involves unrestrained violence designed to produce devastation on a large scale. In the case of "total war," the rules designed to protect civilian populations are callously violated in many respects. Other aspects of "total war" include ethnic cleansing, the utter destruction of landscapes, and strategies aimed at non-combatants, such as starvation blockades. To read Liddell-Hart's argument in full, see B. H. Liddell-Hart, *The Revolution in Warfare* (New Haven: Yale University Press, 1947).

22. Falah, "Israeli-Palestinian War," 257. He notes, "the Israeli strategy of removing the cultural imprint of another group from the landscape is not unique. In post-World War II Czechoslovakia, for example, a similar process of landscape erasure has unfolded." Further, he points to the eradication of German place names, signs, and street templates and – in some instances – tombstones in the Sudetenland was inspired by the desire to eradicate the centuries-long presence of Germans in the area. The Zionist project in Palestine had a similar effect of "denying any Arab historicity in Palestine" by scrubbing the landscape of Palestinian signifiers. See Ted Swedenburg, "The Palestinian Peasant as National Signifier," *Anthropology Quarterly*, 63, no. 1 (January 1990): 19.
23. Diana Taylor, *The Archive and the Repertoire: Performing Cultural Memory in the Americas* (Durham and London: Duke University Press), 2–3.
24. Ghassan Kanafani quoted in Sylomivics, "Bleeding Wound," 19; Hanan Ashrawi quoted in Nassar, "Stories," 16.
25. Hala Kh. Nassar writes, "Palestinian theatre artists constantly question the role of their work. They do so, however, not on the basis of whether it is original or authentic, but rather in terms of what is effective in countering the cultural annihilation under the present occupation." See Nassar, "Stories," 16. However, it is inaccurate to say that all theatre in Palestine aspires to this blunt purpose only. As far back as 1985, the late director Francois Abu-Salem said, "The whole world is not the Palestinian cause, and when you're an artist, you're concerned with many, many other things that happen to humanity. One day, the Palestinians will have a country, and works solely on this narrow subject may be remembered but will no longer have any value." See Ilana DeBare, Lisa Blum, and Francois Abu-Salem, "Palestinian Culture Takes Root," *Journal of Palestine Studies*, 14, no. 23 (1985): 231–2.
26. In her solo performance *Palestine*, Najla Said, daughter of iconic Palestinian scholar Edward Said, dramatizes the opposite diasporic experience of alienation and displacement. Said performed an excerpt from *Palestine* at the New York City Society for Ethical Culture during the protests against the massacre in Gaza

in 2009, describing her entry into Gaza for the first time with her family as a heretofore-pampered teenager. She says, "The car windows are closed but I can smell the open sewage. It feels kind of like we are entering hell ... Despite my mother's insistence that my outfit is fine, I feel very conspicuous and alienated from my people as I descend from the car. I don't think I really feel the intensity of that emotion until I put my fancy, suede shoe down into the muddy earth of Gaza and inhaled that stench." See Najla Said, "Najla Said Reads of Her Teenage Visit to Gaza," YouTube video, 11:42, from a reading and performance at the New York City Society for Ethical Culture, January 13, 2009, www.youtube.com/watch?v=CEMrmRCbvA0& feature=player_embedded.

27. Jajeh, "I Heart Hamas," 19–20.
28. Ibid., 20. Here, Jajeh is also rejecting the notion that – barring national politics – her story might then be recast as a romance: she refuses to be displaced from the center of her own story.
29. Ibid., 21–2.
30. Ibid., 22.
31. Ibid., 27.
32. Najla Said also articulated a desire to escape the baggage of a Palestinian identity by disappearing into another cultural/ethnic/national group when she spoke at the New York Society for Ethical Culture in 2009. She said, "I had a lot of difficulty growing up, dealing with my embarrassing father. And all my Jewish friends, who ... otherwise I fit in [with] perfectly and everyone thought I was Jewish and I got along fine." And in her solo performance *Palestine*, she asks, rhetorically, "Why can't I pass as a Jew if I want? ... Why am I both Arab and American? Why can't I just be one? Why do I have to be aware of suffering and tragedy and cancer and poverty and anger? Why can't I just be normal?" See Said, "Teenage Visit."
33. This scene has been dramatized elsewhere many times in response to occupation. For example, in her performance Scheherazade *Don't Need No Visa*, Laila Farah performs her experience negotiating a series of checkpoints in occupied Lebanon in the 1980s. She writes, "KHALAS!!! Here is your damn paperwork ... I am a dual national you bloody idiot ... Yet when a woman unveils ... tongues start wagging ... Which part of your tongue do I need to chop off?" See Farah, "Dancing," 322.
34. Jajeh says, "When people have complained that the only Israelis I see or speak to in the show are soldiers I tell them: that is who I met while I was there. This is my experience." Jajeh, interview.
35. Jajeh, "I Heart Hamas," 25.

36. Grehan suggests that this term describes the "embodied experiences of individuals and communities as they move (literally and often painfully) across landscapes and homelands." See Helena Grehan, "Rakini Devi: Diasporic Subject and Agent Provocateur," *Theatre Research International*, 28, no. 3 (2003): 229.
37. Farah, "Dancing," 320.
38. Dolan acknowledges the limitations inherent in her construction. She writes, "Utopias can be enforced at the expense of liberty, general consensus achieved by limiting choice. Fascism and utopia can skirt dangerously close to each other." See Jill Dolan, "Performance, Utopia, and the 'Utopian Performative,'" *Theatre Journal*, 53, no. 3 (2001): 457.
39. Grehan, "Rakini Devi," 229.
40. Jajeh, "I Heart Hamas," 32.
41. Ibid., 33.
42. Following the revolutionary events in Egypt, Jajeh inserted an epilogue that takes place during a "Women in Film" event. She has a drink with a man named Michael who expresses doubts about the Arab Spring. Jajeh, incensed, performs her half of the conversation, ending with, "Maybe we should stop trying to force other countries to do what we want and further our own political agenda. Isn't that the definition of terrorism?" See Jajeh, "I Heart Hamas," 33–4.
43. Jajeh, "I Heart Hamas," 33.

14

Doomed by "Dialogue," Saved by Curiosity? Post-9/11 Arab Performances under American Eyes

Margaret Litvin

On Friday, February 20, 2009, the administration of President Barack Hussein Obama was one month old. That day's *Washington Post* covered Hillary Rodham Clinton's first international trip as Secretary of State, a campaign-style "listening tour" of Asia meant to start repairing the United States' image abroad.[1] In Indonesia and Japan, Clinton said she hoped to improve US relations with the Islamic world.[2] In Tokyo, she was photographed with a group of admiring university students, whom she told, "My trip here today is to hear your views."[3]

The same day's *Post* offered sympathetic coverage of the court hearing for Muntadar Al Zaidi, the Iraqi TV journalist who had hurled his shoes at then-President George W. Bush at a press conference two months earlier.[4] In his first public appearance since the shoe-throwing, Al Zaidi stressed the authenticity of his feelings, the legitimacy of his claim to represent his people, and also his journalistic concern for truth:

> "I did not mean to kill the leader of the occupation forces," Muntadar Al Zaidi said, speaking clearly and forcefully from a wooden cage before a packed courtroom. "I was expressing what's inside of me and

what's inside the Iraqi people from north to south and from west to east ... I did not know what achievements [Bush] was talking about [at the press conference] ... I was seeing a million martyrs, seas of Iraqi blood, the desecration of mosques, the raping of Iraqi women and the humiliation Iraqis endure every day, every hour. Because I am a journalist, I know all about that."

The ovation for Al Zaidi, the *Post* noted, was rapturous: "a uniformed Iraqi soldier, apparently moved by the moment, raised his hands in the air and joined the applause" while "women in black *abayas* ululated triumphantly, their high-pitched shrieks reverberating in the courthouse lobby," and the crowd chanted, "Imam Ali is with you, hero!" The hearing, if not the shoe, scored a resounding hit.

Against this background – a new US presidency eager to internationalize its slogans of hope and change in addition to a nearly decade-old habit of heightened American attention to Arab political performances – readers of the Arts & Living section in the same day's *Post* were promised a life-changing treat. Five years in the making, the three-week festival "Arabesque: Arts of the Arab World" was opening at the John F. Kennedy Center for the Performing Arts. "The residents of Washington might not know it yet, but something extraordinary is about to take place on the banks of their [*sic*] Potomac," gushed Ellen McCarthy in a preview titled "Immersed in Arab Culture."[5]

Something that has never before happened here – or anywhere really. Starting Monday, 800 of the finest artists of the vast and varied Arab world will descend on the Kennedy Center for three weeks of unprecedented communion, celebration and cultural exposition ...

It will be a momentous occasion for the artists.

Even more so for us.

Unshackling ourselves from blurry stereotypes and half-formed conceits, we will step into their world without leaving the borders of our city. We'll give ourselves over to the rare and precious opportunity

> to see, hear and taste the flavors of Arab culture through the intimate dialogue exchanged between artist and audience.
>
> The veil is about to be lifted.

The *Post* reader hoping for ironic self-scrutiny would be disappointed: McCarthy's article continues in the same vein, rehashing pernicious clichés ("lifting the veil," "step into their world," "the flavors of Arab culture") even as she hopes to become "unshackled" from stereotyping. Her quotation from Kennedy Center President Michael Kaiser is hardly better. Explaining the festival's rationale in unabashedly US-centric terms, he reifies American ignorance while purporting to challenge it: "[Arabesque is] part of a whole project of the Kennedy Center to bring art about people of whom we know very little, so we can start to understand other people."[6] Beyond this single reporter's puffery, the festival's other public rhetoric also relied on the trope of art as a bridge to understanding between peoples.

It would be easy to deconstruct such rhetoric and mock the self-congratulation it encodes. Any competent cultural critic could argue that such festivals are Orientalist appropriations in effect if not intent, oversimplifying and commodifying the Arab world for American consumption. The evidence abounds: the festival's overambitious 22-country umbrella; the attractive handicraft *souk* in the Kennedy Center basement; the self-serving involvement of Arab embassies (and their kitchens); the title "Arabesque" itself, suggestive of merely decorative flourishes. Going further, one could regard with suspicion the whole phenomenon of American intellectuals' growing *interest* in Arab performance – inextricably tied to US political and military *interests* in the Arab world – over the past decade.

However, in the context of this volume, I want to propose a more hopeful if paradoxical argument: on balance, the expanded American market for Arab-themed performance is a positive development. It has created new spaces (albeit sharply delimited ones) in which Arab artists and American audience members can have conversations enabled and framed but *not* directly mediated by journalistic and academic US-based "experts" on the Middle East. To explore this argument,[7] I will analyze the two major festivals of Arab/Muslim arts held in Washington and New York in 2009. Taken together, these events suggest that the self-representation of Arab artists on American stages – however hackneyed the frames in which they are placed – has given non-academic Americans access to a range of nuanced and potentially thought-provoking representations of Arab realities not easily available to them before and, more importantly, to some exciting new works of art.

In appearing to revive the old-fashioned argument for cultural exchange as a shortcut to understanding between peoples, I do not want to sound naïve. Exchanges, both large-scale arts festivals and "people-to-people" international travel for non-specialists, have been a pillar of superpower foreign policy since the Cold War. Of course the exchange is not neutral. Of course it carries risks: a risk of co-optation for Arab theatre makers tailoring their product to Western markets and a risk of "knowledgeable ignorance" (or eventual disappointment) for American viewers overconfident that they are getting direct and self-interpreting information about the Middle East.[8] These risks must be addressed. Academic preparation can help: festival-goers who have read extensively about the region make better audiences, asking more intelligent questions and allowing artists to tackle more sophisticated subject matter. Like many of my readers, I have dedicated my career to the sort of university teaching that aims to develop more sophisticated audiences for Middle Eastern cultural products, so my comments on "sidelining" academic expertise should be taken with a grain of salt.

Yet one should not exaggerate, either. In the field of academic Middle East studies over about the past 30 years, the barrier to entry has become rather high: in many educated settings, only expert opinions are valued, and undergraduate intuition can be ridiculed as "Orientalizing." The Arab world is now widely considered a "high-context" place[9] that only experts can understand. This, too, can become a form of Orientalization and dehumanization: Arabs become objects of study rather than normal human interlocutors. Academic browbeating can also discourage ordinary Americans (e.g. theatre-goers) from engaging with the region at all. The belief that the Middle East is too complicated to repay engagement can provide another excuse for continued ignorance. While I want to resist the notion that art can or should be politically edifying, I do believe that large mainstream arts festivals, whatever their structural shortcomings, have some educational role here. They can provide openings for American audiences to connect in direct and personally meaningful ways with plays, films, and artists from the Arab world, potentially triggering some questioning of prejudices or even, in the ideal case, inspiring further engagement (reading, travel, language study) with Arabs and Arabic.

Arabesque through the Woodwork

In the spring and summer of 2009, East Coast audiences enjoyed two major festivals of performing arts from the Arab and Muslim worlds. The first, already mentioned, was the 23-day, reputedly $10 million Arabesque festival in Washington from February 23 to March 15. The second was an equally high-profile, ten-day June festival at the Brooklyn Academy of Music in New York, conceived as "Illuminating Islam"[10] but later wisely retitled in the plural: "Muslim Voices: Arts & Ideas." Under the regional and linguistic focus of the first and the religio-cultural focus of the second, each festival sought to highlight both the diversity and the broad appeal of the artistic traditions it chose to represent.

The John F. Kennedy Center for the Performing Arts, located in sedate Foggy Bottom beside the fortress-like Saudi embassy, is the closest thing to a national theatre in the United States. Its previous major festivals had focused on performance traditions from Africa, Latin America, and China. "I become one of America's diplomats doing these festivals," vice president and festival director Alicia Adams later told an interviewer. "We are a quasi-government agency, and usually I'm working with governments."[11] Arabesque's planning proceeded accordingly: the Arab League was enlisted as an official partner; major contributors included the governments of Kuwait and Qatar and the embassy of the United Arab Emirates; additional funding came not only from US foundations and private donors but also Bahrain's Ministry of Culture and Information, Sultan Qaboos Cultural Center (Oman/DC), state-owned Saudi Aramco, and Qatar Foundation, a quango.[12] For these governments and embassies, the festival was an unbeatable public diplomacy opening.

Adams and her colleagues began visiting Arab countries to watch productions and meet Arab artists and intellectuals long before Obama was elected president. They enlisted eminent consultants including Egyptian-British novelist Ahdaf Soueif and Libyan-American poet-translator Khaled Mattawa. They worked to obtain US visas for 800 Arab festival participants. By the summer of 2008, the major performances were in place, and American scholars who offered curatorial or interpretive suggestions (myself included) were politely offered a spot in one of the festival's many accompanying panel discussions or audience talkbacks.

It opened with an element of kitsch, to be sure. The Arab League's pan-Arabist cultural agenda combined with the forces of marketing to produce outreach materials inviting audiences to "unwrap the ... treasures" (more veil-lifting) of a region presented as ancient or even timeless. The materials paid lip service to the Arab world's diversity but immediately subsumed it within a greater, depoliticized, dehistoricized unity – which was then presented as laid bare for American festival-goers:

> Unwrap the cultural treasures of the Arab world in this Kennedy Center international festival showcasing the varied cultures of

> the 22 Arab nations that represent the Arabic-speaking world. From the Arabian Gulf to the Levant to North Africa, this region of the world is the birthplace of human civilization and features extraordinary diversity in geography, traditions, landscape, religion, and contemporary aesthetics. In cooperation with the League of Arab States, the three-week festival brings together artists, many of whom are making their US debut, in performances of music, dance, and theater as well as exhibitions featuring art installations, fashion, a soundscape, cuisine, a marketplace, and much more. Discover the evolution of art forms born from the cradle of human civilization. Experience an amazing breadth of culture that spans both eons and continents.[13]

The festival highlighted some politically non-confrontational exhibits and performances and domesticated some works that were potentially harder-edged. Music and dance were prominent. Designer Azza Fahmy exhibited her jewelry. The Kennedy Center's front hall featured display cases of ornate wedding dresses from various Arab societies, including a few on loan from the private collections of ambassadors' wives. This being Washington, nearby Arab embassies also opened their doors for a "tasting tour" of their respective cuisines on Saturdays during the festival. Meanwhile, a visual arts installation curated by Princess Wijdan Al Hashemi, the Jordanian ambassador to Italy, featured paintings by 26 Arab women artists. The art exhibit was mounted on an elaborate woodwork wall designed to mimic *mashrabiyya*, the latticework decoration used for upper balconies in medieval and Ottoman-era Arab buildings. (Traditionally, *mashrabiyya* carried the connotation of women's space: the lacy woodwork let women observe the street without being seen.) The exhibit bore the self-defeating title (the veil, again) "Breaking the Veils: Women Artists from the Islamic World."[14]

Even these viewer-friendly festival elements are hard to judge too harshly: one can read them as attempting to escape the notion of the Arab world as a region wholly constituted and defined by conflict. But the festival also included serious intellectual engagement. A who's who of Arab writers came in to read or speak on a variety of panels – topics like "Literature and the 'Real' Arab World" or "Migration, Exile, and the Search for Identity" – and many of these auditoriums actually filled up. The Kennedy Center bookstore, more prominent than the basement *souk*, was stocked with an impressive array of Arabic literature in English translation, photography books, and even Arabic-language textbooks and dictionaries. The six documentary and fiction films that were shown included sophisticated offerings from Algeria, Morocco, Lebanon, and Palestine.

Sidestepping Ethnography

Finally, none of the three full-length plays invited to perform – Jalila Baccar's *Khamsoun* (Fifty), Sulayman Al Bassam's *Richard III, an Arab Tragedy*, or Al Kasaba Theatre's *Alive from Palestine* – shied away from politics, even from mildly confronting the US. It is true that all three traveled well: they were already on the international festival circuit before coming to the Kennedy Center. But in view of the warm reception they have enjoyed in the Arab world as well, this can hardly be taken to indicate "made for export" hackery.

As I had argued before seeing the 2009 festivals, such events present a double-edged opportunity for Arab theatre artists. Along with an expanded audience comes the possibility that play-goers are there mainly to be informed about the artist's culture of origin.[15] An audience driven by ethnographic curiosity can turn avant-garde or experimental theatre into the most deadening kind of traditional theatre. Such an audience is ignorant of the local artistic conventions that the experimental work sets out to challenge and against which the theatre maker creates meaning. This audience can misread an individual's creative choices as a mere cultural habit, perhaps something typical of people from that background. It can mistake a stylized or even ironic *appropriation* of a certain cultural tradition – be it a style of dress, music, movement, or speech – for a straightforward part of that tradition. Metaphors are literalized. Satire is misread as fact. Forms of expression which resonated vividly within their original cultural contexts are either mistakenly assumed to be transparent, like journalism, or criticized for being too opaque if a work eludes audience expectations. If the Arab artist derives much of his or her traction and efficacy from a position partly inside and partly outside his or her home culture, the well-meaning Western audience neutralizes that effectiveness by repositioning the artist squarely inside the home culture.[16]

Braving the dangers, at least two of the Kennedy Center's three Arab plays slipped free of their audiences' potential ethnographic expectations. Tunisian theatre-making team Fadhel Jaïbi and Jalila Baccar's *Khamsoun* (2006) explored the roots of Islamist violence in contemporary Tunisia through stylized dance-like sequences and conventional theatre techniques.[17] The play traces the inner journey of a young woman who embraces fundamentalist Islam in France in the wake of the Second Intifada, the September 11 attacks, and the invasion of Iraq. She returns to Tunisia to face skeptical leftist parents, a heavily Islamized society, and brutal police interrogations after her friend, a young female physics teacher, commits a suicide bombing.

Less directly challenging to Western viewers than Baccar's earlier text *Araberlin* (2002),[18] *Khamsoun* premiered at the Odéon in Paris (under the confrontational title *Corps Otages*, or Captive Bodies) and has toured widely. Controversial in the Tunisian and broader Arab contexts – "I produced this play in defense of the values of modernity in Tunisian society and so my daughter won't be forced to wear the headscarf," director Jaïbi has told a Tunisian interviewer[19] – *Khamsoun* risks simply reinforcing European and American viewers' expectations about Islam, religious violence, and the veil. Yet even this work of modernist cultural polemic can surprise the ethnographically curious audience, thematizing history rather than an ahistorical notion of culture. It bristles with hard historical facts that an American audience might not know or not like, as well as graphic scenes of authoritarian government torture. It includes a convinced Islamist as a sympathetic character. Of course, it also illustrates some strains of contemporary Tunisian intellectual debate – an insight quite relevant for Americans seeking to understand the popular uprising in Tunisia a few years later.

Richard III, an Arab Tragedy (2007–09), a Shakespeare adaptation by Kuwaiti-British playwright-director Sulayman Al Bassam, denied the very possibility of such insight.[20] Scornful of the United States' failed meddling in the Middle East, the play opens with the deposed Queen Margaret, who appears carrying a mysterious suitcase (her refugee status, her history, the dismembered body of her dead husband Henry VI) and makes a slap-in-the-face statement to the audience: "You needn't be concerned about me. We lost. It is your right to ignore me. I would ignore myself if my history let me. I don't want your loans, your gifts, your reconstruction grants. I don't want your pity: we lost. All I ask from you is not to question my thirst for revenge."[21] Other aspects of the Kennedy Center production self-consciously mocked Western viewers' attempts to understand, even while offering them a rich and pleasurable quasi-ethnographic portrayal of Gulf Arab society. What they *could* understand did not flatter them. Since *Arab Tragedy*'s Stratford-upon-Avon debut two years earlier, the script had been revised to merge two sinister American characters (the US Ambassador and General Richmond) into the single slovenly character of Mister Richmond (Nigel Barratt), an over-the-top caricature of American ignorance and incompetence.

Perhaps the most controversy-prone (in the American context) work to be invited, Ramallah-based Al Kasaba Theatre's bitterly satirical *Alive from Palestine: Stories under Occupation*, had toured widely, winning Best Production at the Cairo International Festival of Experimental Theatre in 2001.[22] In an earlier US run (New Haven and San Francisco, 2002), reviewers and protestors sometimes mistook the show for a direct journalistic representation of the Palestinian-Israeli conflict.[23] The cautious

Washington Post previewer, too, treated *Alive* as a monotonous agitprop piece, noteworthy only for its "potential of filling an important gap in the topical menu usually available to Washington playgoers."[24] However, *Alive* actually spoofed topicality, starting from the actors' emergence from under a pile of newspapers at the start of the play and continuing through their comic navigation of checkpoints. Rather than the blunt protest play they expected, the sold-out Washington audiences saw wry humor under dehumanizing conditions.[25] As theatre and performance scholar Hazem Azmy has argued, the show "proceeded by means of debunking, in a ... counter-intuitively comedic vein, most of the mass-mediated clichés routinely associated with the Arab-Israeli conflict."[26]

On balance, then, the three plays at the festival challenged American theatre-goers' expectations more than they reinforced them by focusing on history rather than ahistorically understood culture. Albeit less efficiently than Muntadar Al Zaidi's shoe, they quite possibly did contribute to understanding between peoples.

Overall, and keeping in mind the necessary caveats about cultural exchange, I would argue that the tens of thousands of Arabesque attendees – whether American, Arab-American, Arab, or from other parts of Washington's huge international community – did experience aspects of Arab cultures that they would not otherwise know. For the first time in my experience, I heard Arabic spoken inside the Kennedy Center, including by many Arab-American children – evidence of interest in the festival from the Arab immigrant population in the nearby Virginia suburbs. Reaching beyond the attendees, a respected news program in America covered the festival in lengthy segments every night, profiling Arab artists and showcasing their work.[27] For once, Arab cultural production was taken firmly out of the hands of professional Middle East experts – American scholars (like me) who study and explain the Arab world for a living – and in many cases was mediated by Arab writers and artists instead. Some of my colleagues grumbled about the "Orientalist structure" of the festival, but to me the sidelining of academic Middle East Studies opened the way for a more democratic, distinctly non-Orientalist exchange.

In Search of "Muslim Voices"

Smaller in scale but no less eager to break new ground, New York's $2.5 million[28] festival "Muslim Voices: Arts & Ideas" entered the same hopeful political climate, with a fortuitous opening night one day after President Obama's Cairo speech of June 4, 2009. Whereas the inherently and obviously political Washington venue had allowed the Kennedy Center to downplay the Arabesque festival's political thrust, the festival in New York (the cultural capital of the United States) gave politics center stage. Muslim Voices was marketed and received as an explicitly political gesture, a response to the extremism of the Bush years as well as to New York's own 9/11 trauma. BAM President Karen Brooks Hopkins described the festival as conceived in the wake of 9/11 and seriously launched after the 2006 Danish cartoon controversy in an effort to "just bring down the whole level of hostility" around Islam.[29] New York congratulated itself on reclaiming its cosmopolitan open-mindedness. The Empire State Building was lit up with green lights in celebration.[30] The *Village Voice* enthused:

> Dick Cheney is having a hard time letting go, but cowboy diplomacy is on the wane here in the United States – ask President Obama. Nevertheless, the Muslim culture and faith remains misunderstood, at best, and demonized, at worst, by many Americans, so to counter some of those uncertainties and misperceptions, BAM, the Asia Society, and [New York University] NYU's Center for Dialogues are presenting "Muslim Voices: Arts & Ideas," an extensive festival running June 5 to 14.[31]

Quickly channeled by reporters, the festival's rhetoric[32] portrayed the Muslim world as both Other and self, the festival as both an education and a homecoming.[33] Highlighting the presence of "100 Muslim artists from as far away as Indonesia and as nearby as Brooklyn," the *Voice* preview closed, "It's altogether appropriate that this festival is happening in a city once victimized by terrorism. We've seen the worst from the extremists; now it's time to experience the best from the artists."[34] Meanwhile, the *New York Times* celebrated a "Festival for New York, that Muslim City,"[35] and the *Brooklyn Paper* crowed, "New York Finds its Muslim Voice."[36]

Although a few of the artists professed discomfort at the "Muslim voices" framework (some may not have identified as Muslims at all), the performances were generally wholehearted and well received. Organizers were careful to represent as broad a swathe of the Muslim world as they could, not privileging the Arab region. A rousing concert by Senegalese pop star Youssou N'Dour kicked off the festivities; N'Dour also gave a smaller concert at the screening of a documentary film that showcased his "impassioned plea for a more tolerant view of Islam."[37] Other events included dance, music (Sufi, Persian, and Arabic classical music, "oud rock," gospel, hip-hop), film and video screenings, photo exhibits, storytelling, theatre, and more.

To a greater extent than Arabesque, the Muslim Voices festival was burdened by its overt political agenda of "dialogue" between some entity called Islam and another called The West. Here, the presupposition of Islam as monolith – happily banished by the festival's diversity of performances – came back in full force. One of the three organizers (along with BAM and the Asia Society) was the Center for Dialogues, an NYU think tank established after 9/11 for "building bridges of understanding between Islam and the West."[38] Accompanying the performances was a two-day, semi-scholarly conference titled "Bridging the Divide between the United States and the Muslim World through Arts and Ideas: Possibilities and Limitations."[39] The participants, mainly artists, largely ignored this tendentious topic and instead spoke about their own work.

Was the Muslim Voices festival preaching to the (enlightened, Western) choir? Was it, further, an act of self-assertion by liberal New Yorkers? During the performance of Al Bassam's *Richard III, an Arab Tragedy*, which headlined this festival as well, the Brooklyn audience chortled at the US-directed political jokes (e.g., Emir Gloucester's line about driving "the world to war with PowerPoint") as had the Washington audience. They were intrigued by the production's use of Islamic signifiers and its pessimistic ending. But it was the post-show Q&A (which I moderated) that briefly took them out of their comfort zone: one nervous-looking man in the front row stood up to stammer a question about what he called the play's "negative portrayal of Americans ... after we've done so much for those people over there." An alarmed tremor went through the auditorium, then furious whispering. Audience members began heckling and booing the questioner even before he had finished and before Al Bassam had begun to answer. A BAM organizer later told me she had been momentarily afraid the man would commit some act of violence. Ironically, at a festival so dedicated to "dialogue," she and the audience behaved as though dissenting views, however naïve, contained an inherent threat.

Representing Arabs and Muslims

Let me tease out some of the apparent contradictions in the argument I've proposed. The skeptic says: it is not art's job to teach or edify, and artists can even be corrupted by playing to audiences whose curiosity is ethnographic or forensic. The optimist says: events like Arabesque and (perhaps to a lesser extent) Muslim Voices actually can expand audiences' knowledge of Arab or Muslim realities, and this is a good thing. Likewise, the skeptic says: organized efforts to promote "dialogue" with "the Other" through art are doomed, because they must begin by reifying the Other into a single addressable interlocutor.[40] And yet, the optimist retorts: isolated small moments of dialogic give-and-take sometimes do emerge – although they more often fail to emerge, as in the "deaf dialogue" Brooklyn Q&A described above – from particular play-goers' encounters with particular performances. The skeptic says: the box is Orientalist, how could it not be? And yet, the optimist says: there are wonderful things inside.

At various times and in different roles, I have argued for different sides of this debate. To a professional scholar's ears, the optimist above sounds dated and bizarre: how very 1990s to think a work of art can or should cure anyone's misconceptions of the Other, and how very 1790s to think it might deepen anyone's soul! And yet this view still captures some of our intuitions as language learners, dramaturgs, translators, and teachers – or why would we bother? The optimist offers more scope for creative action, even if the skeptic is right.

One graceful approach to this knot is a performance that explicitly thematizes the unknowability of other people, their cultures, and, more importantly, their histories. As a rejoinder to Queen Margaret's speech in Sulayman Al Bassam's *Richard III*, quoted above, let me close with an example from an American play dealing with the same events (the war in Iraq) and the same theme: the invading army's inability to know its victims' lives.

American playwright Quiara Alegría Hudes's *Elliot, a Soldier's Fugue* (2006) is part of a new wave of American and British plays in the past decade that have engaged *not* primarily with Arab cultures but with the British and American wartime conscience. These plays have a complicated relationship with current events. As leftist playwright and anthologist Karen Malpede argues, "Written in the midst of unfolding history, ... these are plays that let the present in."[41] Yet it is also true, as British literary scholar Suman Gupta argued in his recent book *Imagining Iraq*, that plays about the Iraq War, especially the tribunal-like verbatim dramas, have "participated in the effort to provide closure of the Iraq invasion period."[42]

Elliot, a Soldier's Fugue (2006) includes no Arab or Muslim characters at all; in its baroque tangle of voices – its governing metaphor is the fugue – none pretends to represent the Other. Instead the focus is on probing the self, its own history. Whereas most American "Iraq plays" have fallen more or less unconsciously into the tradition of Vietnam protest theatre,[43] Hudes foregrounds and explores the relationship between America's two disastrous wars. Her Puerto Rican-American character Elliot is haunted not only by the memories of killing and being wounded but also by the family history that has driven him to enlist: his father and mother served in Vietnam, his flute-playing grandfather in Korea. "Pop, we lived the same fucking life," he says.[44] Nor is Vietnam, for this family, as radically foreign as one might expect: Elliot's nurse mother Ginny finds that its mountains, seen from the window of her hospital, "look like views of Puerto Rico."[45]

In one of the play's deeply moving "fugue" scenes, Pop in Vietnam and Elliot in Iraq simultaneously make their first kills. The scene opens simply: "The empty space. Two wallets are on the ground."[46] These wallets represent the enemy targets: one Viet Cong and the other an armed Iraqi. The audience never sees these men's faces or hears their stories or learns whether they were actually participating in an insurgency; no Arabic words and only a few words of Vietnamese are spoken during the whole play. One might think this would amount to a silencing or elision, yet again, of Arab voices from a play about Iraq. Yet as we watch Pop and Elliot bend over the two wallets, now representing the dead men with their referent-less identities, dog tags, and family photos, we imagine what they have seen.

Hudes's haunting image – the Iraqi corpse represented only by a wallet on the ground – offers one dark answer to the question of how much American theatre can represent or US audiences can understand. The wallet is the twin, from the opposite perspective, of Queen Margaret's suitcase in Al Bassam's

Richard III. Honestly representing the Other, the wallet implies, is not about staging a dialogue, studying or even respecting his or her culture, or learning to decode the identity documents or parse the photographs. It may be simply about acknowledging that such contents and contexts exist before proceeding to explore one's own as deeply and poetically as possible.

Notes

1. Glenn Kessler, "On Asia Trip, Clinton Shows How She'll Try to Repair the U.S. Image Around the World," *Washington Post*, February 20, 2009, www.washingtonpost.com/wp-dyn/content/article/2009/02/19/AR2009021903471.html?sid=ST2009021903526.
2. Ibid.
3. Ibid.
4. Ernesto Londoño and Zaid Sabah, "Shoe-Throwing Iraqi Defends Attack on Bush; Jailed Journalist Says He Found President's Manner Infuriating," *Washington Post*, February 20, 2009.
5. Ellen McCarthy, "Critic's Picks: Arabesque: Arts of the Arab World: Immersed in Arab Culture," *Washington Post*, February 20, 2009.
6. Ibid.
7. I am grateful to Eyad Houssami for his insight and encouragement and to the two anonymous readers for their perceptive comments.
8. On "knowledgeable ignorance," see Ziauddin Sardar and Merryl Wyn Davies, *Why Do People Hate America?* (Cambridge: Icon, 2002), 12, 160. The term was coined in Norman Daniel, *Islam and the West: The Making of an Image* (Edinburgh: Edinburgh University Press, 1966).
9. I am slightly extending anthropologist Edward T. Hall's definition of a "high-context culture," in which outsiders understand less because more is left unsaid. See Edward T. Hall, *Beyond Culture* (Garden City, NY: Anchor Press, 1976). The notion of "high-context" is still used, for instance, in research on Arabic pedagogy. See Karin C. Ryding, "New Alignments, New Discourses," *Profession* (2008): 214–18.
10. It is thus identified on the websites of donor organizations, including: Rockefeller Brothers Fund, "Brooklyn Academy of Music, Inc., Grant Detail," accessed October 12, 2011, www.rbf.org/grant/11534/brooklyn-academy-music-inc-0; Doris Duke Charitable Foundation, "DDFIA Building Bridges Program, New

York, NY," accessed October 12, 2011, www.shangrilahawaii.org/DDFIA/Building-Bridges-Program/Grants-Awarded.
11. Nelson Pressley, "The Kennedy Center's Alicia Adams Brings the World to D.C. Stages," *Washington Post*, February 25, 2011.
12. Kennedy Center, "Arabesque: Arts of the Arab World," accessed October 12, 2011, www.kennedy-center.org/programs/festivals/08-09/arabesque.
13. Ibid. (English text and Arabic translation.)
14. For details on the exhibition, which had been at the Clinton Library in Arkansas and other venues, see Kelly P. Kissel, "Exhibit of Works from Islamic Women Aims to Shatter Stereotypes," Associated Press, 2008, http://hosted.ap.org/specials/interactives/_arts/islamic_women.
15. This paragraph draws on my presentation at the Cairo International Festival of Experimental Theatre in 2008.
16. The corrupting influence of ethnographic interest exists in literature as well; Iraqi poet, novelist, and literature professor Sinan Antoon has aptly termed it "forensic interest": "Life for a displaced Arab writer, if you want to, if you're willing to exoticise yourself and self-orientalize, life is very good and very profitable," Antoon told an interviewer. "I don't want to be the native informant ... There is increased interest in the Arab world. But I call it forensic interest. For the most part it's bad because it's assumed that novels and poems are going to explain September 11 to you ... I am against that kind of interest, and I am always in support of writers who debunk that kind of interest and confuse the reader." See Ed Lake, "Sinan Antoon: 'I Don't Want to be the Native Informant,'" *The National* (Abu Dhabi), March 4, 2010. (I am grateful to Marcia Lynx Qualey for the reference.) For Jorge Luis Borges's related argument that "what is truly native can and often does dispense with local color," just as the Quran largely dispenses with camels, see Jorge Luis Borges, "The Argentine Writer and Tradition," *Labyrinths: Selected Stories & Other Writings* (New York: New Directions, 1964), 181.
17. See the (unfortunately titled) *Post* review: Celia Wren, "Tunisian Culture Laid Bare, in 'Khamsoun,' at the Kennedy Center," *Washington Post*, March 16, 2009.
18. See Jalila Baccar, *Araberlin* (Paris: Editions Théâtrales, 2003). In English in Marvin Carlson, ed., *Four Plays from North Africa* (New York: Martin E. Segal Theatre Center Publications, 2008).
19. For more on Jaïbi's ultimately successful battle with the Tunisian Ministry of Culture's censorship office, see Jamel Arfaoui, "Tunisian Director Refuses to Censor Play," *Magharebia*, November 17, 2006, www.magharebia.com/cocoon/awi/xhtml1/en_GB/features/awi/features/2006/11/17/feature-01.

20. See Al Bassam's essay in this volume. See also Margaret Litvin, "*Richard III, an Arab Tragedy* (review)," *Shakespeare Bulletin*, 25, no. 4 (2007): 85–91; Margaret Litvin, "Explosive Signifiers: Sulayman Al-Bassam's Post 9/11 Odyssey," *Shakespeare Yearbook*, 18 (2010): 105–39.
21. Sulayman Al Bassam, "Richard III, an Arab Tragedy" (unpublished Arabic and English playscripts, 2007).
22. For Al Kasaba's other international presentations, see the company's website: Al Kasaba Theatre, "International Participations," accessed October 12, 2011, www.alkasaba.org/details.php?id=grjhdua1554yhpn15e10r.
23. See Charles McNulty, "The New World Border: International Theater in the Post-9-11 Era," *Village Voice*, July 9, 2002; and Robert Hurwitt, "Palestinians Tell Their Side in 'Alive'," review of *Alive from Palestine: Stories under Occupation* by Al Kasaba Theatre, *San Francisco Chronicle*, July 9, 2002.
24. Peter Marks, "Theater: Alive from Palestine," *Washington Post*, February 8, 2009.
25. Nelson Pressley, "Theater Review: 'Alive from Palestine: Stories under Occupation' at the Kennedy Center," *Washington Post*, February 28, 2009.
26. Hazem Azmy, "Staging Egypt on the Global Stage: (De)Constructing Narratives of Post-9/11 Egyptian Performance Realities" (PhD dissertation draft, University of Warwick, 2011), prologue. Manuscript of draft prologue kindly shared by Hazem Azmy.
27. NewsHour's opening report can be heard at PBS NewsHour, "Arabesque Opens at the Kennedy Center," February 24, 2009, www.pbs.org/newshour/art/blog/2009/02/arabesque-opens-at-the-kennedy-center.html.
28. Melik Kaylan, "Muslim Voices, Western Ears," *Wall Street Journal*, June 17, 2009.
29. Nikola Krastev, "New York Arts Festival Aims to Dispel Misconceptions About Islam," Radio Free Europe/Radio Liberty, June 12, 2009.
30. For the building's lighting policy, see Official Site of the Empire State Building, "Tower Lights," accessed October 12, 2011, www.esbnyc.com/current_events_tower_lights.asp.
31. Tad Hendrickson, "Youssou N'Dour Headlines BAM's Ambitious, Overdue 'Muslim Voices' Festival," *Village Voice* (New York), June 3, 2009.
32. See Muslim Voices: Arts & Ideas, "Festival," accessed October 12, 2011, http://muslimvoicesfestival.org/about/festival.
33. The coverage is collected at Muslim Voices: Arts & Ideas, "Media Coverage," accessed October 12, 2011, http://muslimvoicesfestival.org/press/press-coverage.
34. Hendrickson, "Youssou N'Dour."

35. Felicia R. Lee, "Festival for New York, that Muslim City," *New York Times*, June 4, 2009.
36. Evan Gardner, "BAM finds its Muslim voice," *Brooklyn Paper* (New York), May 28, 2009.
37. BAM, "Youssou N'Dour: I Bring What I Love," accessed October 12, 2011, www.bam.org/view.aspx?pid=1136
38. http://islamuswest.org.
39. For details and conference footage, see Muslim Voices: Arts & Ideas, "About the Conference," accessed October 12, 2011, http://muslimvoicesfestival.org/about/conference.
40. As I have argued elsewhere: Margaret Litvin, review of *Veiled Monologues*, by Adelheid Roosen, *Ecumenica*, 1, no. 2 (special issue, "Performing Islam/Muslim Realities") (2008): 120–2.
41. K. Malpede, M. Messina, and B. Shuman, eds., *Acts of War: Iraq and Afghanistan in Seven Plays* (Evanston, IL: Northwestern University Press, 2011).
42. Suman Gupta, *Imagining Iraq: Literature in English and the Iraq Invasion* (Basingstoke: Palgrave Macmillan, 2011), 118.
43. A comparison I hope to explore elsewhere.
44. Quiara Alegría Hudes, *Elliot, a Soldier's Fugue* (New York: Dramatists Play Service, 2007), 36.
45. Ibid., 27.
46. Ibid., 21.

15

Remembering Saadallah Wannous

Jawad Al Asadi

As Arab theatre calcifies, fractures, and disintegrates, the legacy and repertoire of Saadallah Wannous bestrides the chasm of pain and hope and beams through a portal to the past. His work forged a path that traverses bitter embers to his dark, turbulent era. When bearers of enlightenment fall, when modernizers take their own lives, when rationalists emigrate from ruined lands, Wannous swings his pickaxe, chipping away at the collective psyche and challenging the masses with his ideas. He draws from the wellspring of his circumstances, and he stones the evils of his age. Few intellectuals share this quixotic mission to reignite the spin of windmills – frozen by defeat, ossified by regression – even if only to claim the chimera of victory, an impossible conquest under Arab authoritarianism, a political order of incontrovertible illegitimacy.

Wannous's theatre excavates, awakens, and recreates what has been lost. It pieces together shards of woe, ruin, and pain, discarded on the pavement. Wannous saw the world from an ever-shifting perspective, never caving in to empty rhetoric, dogma, or manufactured ideas. Instead, he restored, instigated, and reconfigured, never repeating himself or what others had done, never mimicking the West. He drew from the distinctive here and now. He absorbed his present, digested it, and then gave it back to us as a means of restoring the infinitude of consciousness against all odds. In his play *Ritual for a Metamorphosis* (1994) and his text *Evanescent Death* (1996), Wannous strips away pretense and ideology to unleash free and radiant truths in the tradition of Anton Chekhov, Luigi Pirandello, and Jean Genet.

In his final piece, *Evanescent Death*,[1] Wannous places readers in the vortex of inferno. A culmination of his life's work, *Death* is a declaration of pain, regret, and anguish – a living, breathing carnival of language that brutally addresses the conditions and realities of his era and of today. Wannous kicks up dust, bares the latent tumors underneath our skin, chipping away at the estrangement of place and character. His last plays and texts are more open than his previous work, pushing readers and audiences down forbidden paths, into off-limit spaces, towards uninhibited lust.

While the characters of his repertoire – Moumina, Rahil, The Singer, Jabr, Ibn Khaldoun – are deeply rooted in the tradition of Arab philosophy, Wannous subverts the substantive and metaphysical architecture of historical texts in order to reconstruct and impart them to the present. He does so through storytelling magic and lends the texts a dimension of enlightenment, feminine or masculine in a lovesick, tortured rhythm – an enlightenment living on a double-edged hope of awakening to horror, of horror born by the awakened.

In his play *Rape* (1990), Wannous situates the narrow-sighted Jewish characters – Golda Meir, Sara Benhas, and Gideon Hausner – in a minefield of hostile confrontations. The play reveals their hostile inflexibility and the fragility of Palestinian hope, which has fallen so deeply into the abyss of rhetoric, of ruin and delusion. His play *The Adventures of Jabr the Mamluk's Head* (1970), a story about the wild lust for power and wealth, deploys legendary Baghdadi poetics to convey the pain of Baghdad's people and their dreams of freedom.

* * *

How do we handle the texts of Wannous today? What distinguishes any work of dramatic literature? Do we maintain and actualize words and semiotics exactly as they are on the printed page, or do we push the text to alternative possibilities? Is the director the only mediator of text? Or do texts, in the hands of directors, transcend their own limits, pivot towards uncharted horizons, and open to unexpected and latent visual beauty? On the one hand, directors may choose to consecrate the text and to stage it as literally as possible, merely singing or reciting it, a pure transmission from the tongues of the actors. On the other hand, directors may exercise their creative liberty as the Russian director Yuri Lubimov did with *Hamlet*, reinterpreting the Shakespearean text by casting famous Russian singer and bard Vladimir Vysotsky, who performed the role for nearly nine consecutive years in Moscow's Taganka Theatre until his death in 1980.

Critics described the director's interpretation as satanic and audacious: the text ventured to the unexpected, and the spirit of Lubimov's directing and Vysotsky's performance became forged upon the structure of *Hamlet*. Could we – or even Shakespeare, for that matter – have imagined that Hamlet would fill Moscow with the beauty of Vysotsky's voice? Could we have anticipated that the existential questions would be conveyed by a Russian singer who so fully absorbed Shakespeare's text that he became its author?

The relationship between the director and the text develops to the point where the ways in which a director reads and challenges the text to explore new questions, semiotics, and visions will become as important to the text's journey from the page to the stage as the literal interpretation and staging.

* * *

Saadallah Wannous's texts derive from a hunger and thirst to reveal the heart of oppression, a search for the roots of pretense, regression, and spiritual defeat. His work does not wear the mask of ambiguity but rather pins down the root of bitterness and of clashing desires. His texts, inspired by Bertolt

Brecht, portray contexts more than they delve into the depths of characters. In that regard, Wannous's repertoire tends to modernize the search for the internal mask of characters.

Wannous's interest in Brecht was built on a sense of intellectual and professional belonging to a literary tradition that addresses the political foundations of our existence first and the human experience second. Wannous was indelibly marked by Brecht. It was not an experimental tendency nor due to similar mindsets. Wannous's theatrical manifestos and the tenants he lays out in the introductions to his texts demonstrate the political, politicized, and politicizing objectives of playwriting, a practice of the intellect and of storytelling.

His plays *The King is King* (1977), *Soirée for the 5th of June* (1968), *The Elephant, the King of All Time* (1969), and to a lesser extent *The Adventures of Jabr the Mamluk's Head* reveal how Wannous began to shift his focus to human narratives, to delve into characters without falling into the trap of donning an ideological mask. *Jabr the Mamluk*, in particular, signaled a transition from political rhetoric to deeper human content. In *Ritual for a Metamorphosis*, Wannous does away in large part with ideological rhetoric and favors instead real engagement with what makes us human. While *Ritual* exposes the political mechanics of society and power, the play sanctifies humanity and its existential questions.

This is evident in the character of the Mufti, a Muslim religious leader. This *Ritual* character is a rational thinker who poses philosophical questions about his sociopolitical circumstances and the depths of his own soul, much like Hamlet. The Mufti probes mysteries, intentions, and desires of his mind, body, and soul, long covered in dust. We all share with the Mufti the longing to purge ourselves of the putrid legacy of authoritarianism. He represents our collective desire to strip ourselves down to the core, to discover who we are. The actor who performs the Mufti must provide more than still, dry acting. This character requires a Hamletian actor, with a manic soul, a quivering voice, a trembling heart, an actor who toes the line of inferno. The Mufti merits exceptional attention because he is the entirety of the text. A dry, rough performance that is not manic burns the entire text.

From the playwriting process to the performance of a scene by actors, the journey of a theatrical text is complex. It is a process of transformation, deconstruction, interpretation, embodiment, and transcendence. When does the deconstruction of a dramatic text constitute betrayal? How do you go about sanctifying a text, remaining loyal to it, then slaughtering it? How does the writer relate to his text, and vice versa? How do the literary influences of a playwright come to light in performance? Is the text all there is to performance, or is it merely one component of theatre? Does a director have the right to a different reading, or should playwrights be assured literal interpretations of their texts? What is the role of the actor in these divergent processes of literal interpretation or of transformation?

* * *

Saadallah Wannous taught death a lesson it will never forget. I confess, I felt awe and panic at the thought of Saadallah Wannous's journeying into the unknown of the hereafter. In his last month, I couldn't pick up the phone and call him. I avoided his pictures in the press, I avoided speaking his name. I was scared, scared for him, for myself. It was a bitter, traumatic experience, as if I carried him with me, on my shoulders, inside of me, in my blood. He consumed my entire being, and yet I was afraid to reach out to him. It was a dual sensation of loss, of excluding him from my life and pulling him towards me.

The time we spent together always transported me from the present. The first years of our friendship were as volcanic as they were sweet and fresh. We sat at a table in the Al Qabbani Theatre in Damascus discussing texts and words. We decided on props, costumes, and lighting ahead of the first rehearsals for his play *The Adventures of Jabr the Mamluk's Head*. He attended rehearsals with childish humor, with a perceptive and alert intellect, with eagerness and nostalgia. It felt like I was living through the years of his first endeavors. We split the apple of theatre. He was the master of text, the architect, and I ushered the text onto the stage through directing. For Wannous, rehearsals were paradise. He entranced the actors, loved them, drove them to deep introspection, and sparked debate. He made rehearsals the pinnacle of the sublime, the heights of spiritual pleasure. He was never satisfied. He had the gift of penetrating foresight. His knowledge, his perception of time, his archaeology of the past – they resulted in a sculpture that fused both the harrowing intimacy and the delight of alienation in theatre. His work reaches into the well of history and re-establishes it to serve the present.

Wannous was a sculptor – at once of this earth, of the future, of the spirit. He exemplified his longing for a life more open to enlightenment.

* * *

The crammed alleys of Damascus, brimming with friendliness, brought us together. We imbibed the holiest of holy waters until we toasted to the sacred texts of God! As I continue to wander, I feel that he exists now and tomorrow, that he lives in me, with me, that I am of him and live in him. I refuse to accept that he has left us forever. It is more probable that Wannous rented a drunken skiff and sailed away from this dark, cruel earth. He wanted to sail away in his skiff across the fathomless seas to forget bitterness, if only for a moment. Wannous knew how to defeat death. He knew how to teach death a lesson. His writing is a final vindication of life. Just as his last plays revealed the corruption of the powers-that-be and denuded society to unveil its hypocrisy, so too were they doomed by hope, by the anthem of the spirit yearning for freedom.

* * *

Pain is the essence of the soul, the immunity of meaning, a virgin paradise, the pleasure of introspection, the gates of mourning, the pickaxe that unleashes springs in texts, the hallmark of resistance, inscriptions of absence, loneliness in desolation.

When my mother bid me farewell upon my departure from Baghdad, she expected me to return and didn't realize the gravity of the situation, that I would not see home again, that I would not set foot on the sidewalks or drink from the Tigris or the Euphrates. She did not know where I would sleep or in what shelter I would hide. My car headed towards Damascus, crossing the border with Iraq. At that time, Damascus meant only one thing to me. It meant Saadallah Wannous.

After years of joking around, disagreements, and reconciliations, Wannous's home became a part of who I was. When my mother visited me in Damascus, I took her on a pilgrimage to Wannous's house before we visited the Sayyida Zainab shrine. At the shrine, she cried and pulled on the grating, embraced it, imploring God to protect me and Wannous. She got us strips of green fabric to wrap around our wrists as if we were making a vow. She put the green strips in our hands, kissed Wannous's head, and said to him, "Look after my son."

I passed the evenings in Wannous's home, his smile warm, imbuing his speech with congeniality as we ruminated on theatre, theatre in ruins and ruinous plays. We, along with other collaborators, spelled out our dreams. We sketched them out, put them on paper. Wannous proposed plays for the season at the Al Qabbani Theatre. He marveled at *Danton's Death* (1835) and *Woyzeck* (1837) by Georg Büchner, and *Richard III*, which he considered the most effective text to satirize Arab dictatorship. He proposed plays that resonated with modern Arab audiences, and in our discussions he never forgot, nor have we since, the role of aesthetics in enhancing performance. It was as if we were living in an endless dream, as if our homes were workshops, festivals, sites of theatrical euphoria.

How can I imagine Syrian or Arab theatre without Saadallah Wannous? Or Saadallah Wannous without theatre? Step by step, bit by bit, with intent, like an enthralled child or patient priest, Wannous sat at his desk in the Al Qabbani Theatre in the company of friends and students. Debate was fiery, opinions clashed and exchanged while he registered our condition of collapse, of defeat.

There was a hellish ten years when Wannous did not write a single word. Ten years of estrangement, desperation, and bitterness towards the Arab governmental theatre institutions. Ten years of controversy and a violent struggle with the Self and the world. Wannous understood and knew how to take in the desolation, not only to digest it, but to rewrite it – not only as a playwright, but as an unrivalled intellectual. I have never seen or felt passion as fiery or immediate as Saadallah Wannous's, especially when it came to questions of nationalism and defining historical moments.

On that ominous morning, when Baghdad became a field of fire and air raids, on the day when the tanks, like iron buffalos, raided my homeland and my people, Wannous cried and screamed and beat his head against the walls. He said to me, "They're burning my people. They're tearing down my house over my head. Baghdad!" he screamed. "Baghdad!" he cried.

He was neither a spectator nor a passive bystander to the historical events of his era and to the causes of his people. Palestine coursed through his veins, and Damascus was in his heart. He always defended civil society and civic understanding as well as implementing democracy, strengthening constitutions, combating demagogues. He charted a course towards a society free from oppression and desperation. His last texts, from *Ritual* to *Death*, broach untouchable subjects and probe unspoken taboos. Perhaps Wannous's greatest achievement was writing texts that affirm life in the face of death. Writing bounded him to existence, a way of being neither weak nor withdrawn nor defeated, a victorious existence.

Translated by Meris Lutz

Note

1. Published as a novella in Arabic and also translated to French, this text interweaves episodes of memoir and playwriting. Wannous wrote the text towards the end of his five-year period living with cancer. He completed *Evanescent Death* in August 1996, shortly before his death in May 1997.

Contributor Biographies

Jawad Al Asadi is an Iraqi theatre director, playwright, and the founder and director of Babel Theatre in Beirut, Lebanon.

Sulayman Al Bassam is a writer, performer, and director of theatre based in Kuwait, where he runs an independent production company, SABAB Theatre, with his collaborator Georgina Van Welie.

Abdullah Al Kafri is a writer, dramaturg, journalist, and cultural manager, and his plays include *Damascus-Aleppo*, *Mrs. Ghada's Threshold for Pain*, *Colorful Noise*, *Visitor's Permit*, and *Half a Gram of Pink Meat*.

Asaad Al-Saleh is an assissant professor of comparative literature and cultural studies at the University of Utah.

Meisoun Ali is a professor at the High Institute of Dramatic Arts in Damascus, Syria.

Dalia Basiouny is an Egyptian writer, theatre artist, and academic, and she teaches theatre at the American University in Cairo, Egypt.

Zeina Daccache is a Lebanese actress, director, drama therapist, and the founding director of Catharsis – Lebanese Center for Drama Therapy.

Samia Habib is an Egyptian cultural critic and university professor.

Katherine Hennessey holds a PhD in English, with a concentration in Irish theatre, from the University of Notre Dame in the United States and has lived in Sanaa, Yemen, since 2009.

Eyad Houssami makes and writes about theatre and culture, and he is the founding director of Masrah Ensemble, a nonprofit theatre organization based in Lebanon.

Rania Jawad is a PhD candidate in the Department of Middle Eastern and Islamic Studies at New York University, and she currently teaches drama and literature at Birzeit University, Palestine.

Elias Khoury is a Lebanese writer and public intellectual, and his novels include *Little Mountain, The Journey of Little Ghandi, Yalo, As Though She Were Sleeping,* and *Sinalkol.*

Margaret Litvin is an assistant professor of Arabic and comparative literature at Boston University and the author of *Hamlet's Arab Journey.*

Rabih Mroué is an actor and theatre director from Beirut whose plays include *Three Posters*, *Looking for a Missing Employee*, *Who's Afraid of Representation?*, and *Photo Romance.*

Joseph Shahadi is a performance/theatre artist and scholar, and he earned a PhD in Performance Studies from New York University.

Edward Ziter is an associate professor in the Department of Drama at New York University and affiliated faculty in the Departments of English and Performance Studies, and he is the author of *The Orient on the Victorian Stage* and currently at work on a monograph on Syrian theatre.

Photographers

Yazan Khalili is an architect, visual artist, and writer who lives and works in, around, and out of Palestine.

Dalia Khamissy is a photographer based in Beirut, and her work, which revolves around social and political issues, has been exhibited and published internationally.

Joseph Seif is a photographer, cinematographer, and director based in San Francisco.

The following photographs in the plates section are by Dalia Khamissy: 1 and 2, 4–15, and 17. Photographs 3 and 16 were taken by Yazan Khalili and Joseph Seif, respectively.